D0375383

Lighten Up and Enjoy Life More

Lighten Up and Enjoy Life More

Everyday Ways to De-stress Your Lifestyle

Margaret Houk

Judson Press ® Valley Forge

Lighten Up and Enjoy Life More: Everyday Ways
to De-stress Your Lifestyle
© 1996 by Margaret Houk
Published by Judson Press, Valley Forge, PA 19482-0851

All rights reserved. No part of this publication may be reproduced, stored
in a retrieval system, or transmitted in any form or by any means, elec-
tronic, mechanical, photocopying, recording, or otherwise, without the prior
permission of the copyright owner, except for brief quotations included in a
review of the book.
Bible quotations in this volume are from the NEW REVISED STAND-
ARD VERSION of the Bible, copyrighted 1989 by the Division of Christian
Education of the National Council of the Churches of Christ in the United
States of America, and are used by permission.
"A Morning Resolve," by Bishop Vincent from *A Pocket Prayer Book and*
Devotional Guide, Ralph Spaulding Cushman, © 1941, 1969, published by
The Upper Room, 1908 Grand Avenue, P. O. Box 189, Nashville, TN 37202.
Used by permission of the publisher.
Poem by Sue Wall reprinted from Ann Landers, in the *Post-Crescent*
(Appleton, WI), July 8, 1994. Used by permission.

Library of Congress Cataloging-in-Publication Data
Houk, Margaret, 1932-
    Lighten up and enjoy life more : everyday ways to de-stress your life-
style / Margaret Houk.
        p. cm.
    ISBN 0-8170-1240-0 (pbk. : alk. paper)
    1. Women—Religious life. 2. Women—Conduct of life. 3. Stress man-
agement. I. Title.
BV4527.H686 1996
248.8'43—dc20   95-50510

Printed in the U.S.A.
05 04 03 02 01 00 99 98 97 96
10 9 8 7 6 5 4 3 2 1

To him
for whom I live each day

Contents

Acknowledgments

Special thanks are due my favorite working moms, my daughters Cindy, Debbie, and Sue, for their helpfulness and suggestions in preparing the material for this book.

Accolades and my abundant gratitude go to my writer's critique group—Beth Ziarnik, Linda DeVries, and Pat Kohls—for the many hours they spent editing this manuscript and pointing out welcome improvements.

My heartfelt appreciation needs to be sent to the editorial staff at Judson Press, whom I have found to be caring and who have welcomed me and included me in the exciting publishing process.

1

You Can Make It Happen!

Are you one of those people who wake up to an alarm, bound out of bed with a reluctant bang, and rush like mad to get ready for work—all the while hassling the kids to get dressed, fed, and off to school? You dart through traffic and hustle through a full day of work, only to come home to cook supper, run one child to swim class, help another with her homework, and try to squeeze in the laundry or shopping that you didn't get done over the weekend.

In between, you glance at the daily news so you can keep up with what's going on in the world. Occasionally you make it, but you know you're missing something now and then. In your spare time (what is *that*?), you try to read up on the latest health, nutrition, and environmental concerns, as well as child-care techniques so you can do a good job of living and parenting. You love your job and adore the children (and, if married, your husband), but you wonder when the fun part starts.

Or you may be an at-home mother or volunteer having time-stress problems. Many at-home moms and volunteers are as busy as their friends in the working world. The only difference is that their hectic pace is caused by chasing a toddler most of each day or finding time in their lives for their home and family plus school library duty and Red Cross meetings.

Or you may be a single working adult or a retired person.

1

You don't have the responsibilities of raising children, but your job demands, needs for companionship, or pressing requests for volunteer help send you down the same slippery paths.

What is there about modern life . . .

You pray when you can, to keep in touch with God and His will. Your prayers include requests to find the time to enjoy life more. But nothing ever seems to change.

Life Is Complex

Life in our world today is complex and becoming more so. The late twentieth century has brought us busy, noisy urban and suburban living, jobs outside the home, appliances and cars that break down, dogs that bark (and, for marrieds, husbands who don't, when the children need disciplining), budgets that run up too fast, and vacations that resemble more a visit to the fun house than a leisurely retreat. In addition, we modern women are beset on every side with calls to lose weight, recycle, exercise, clean the stove, care for others, and still take good care of ourselves. In short, to be Superwoman.

We are also advised to reduce the excess stress in our lives, but nobody has yet found a magic formula for doing that. (I secretly suspect that the people who give out that advice go home at the end of the day as frazzled as we are.) We really can't complain, because life has never been as comfortable for the masses as it is today in Western civilized countries. But modern life, late-twentieth-century style, has brought with it a lot of anxiety.

I think we can do something about that. We can do so without resorting to such technical helps as behavior modification training or tranquilizers. "There is nothing new under the sun," the wise Solomon said. Our basic human needs and wants haven't really changed over the centuries. They've just shifted in form. And perhaps, in recent years, in intensity.

What people want, and have always wanted, is a meaningful life enriched with loving relationships. Many of us have that today. The trouble is, we don't have time to sit back, appreciate, and enjoy it.

Several reasons have been given for the time shortage. Erma Bombeck says it's "the frantic pace of people wanting to be all things to all people and doing everything before they are 30." A noted academic, David J. Ward, blames it on increasingly stressful job conditions brought on by falling real wages, foreign competition, and the rising cost of fringe benefits, particularly health care. Douglas John Hall, a professor of Christian theology, suggests "the religion of progress" is at fault—the unrealistic belief that the next generation would always be healthier, wealthier, and wiser than the one before it.

There Is an Answer

Whatever the cause, there is a remedy. We can de-stress our lifestyles by gradually acquiring more and more "easy-living" thoughts, attitudes, and habits. With time and effort, we can even reach a point of relative ease and comfort.

How do I know? Because I have done it. I have, over time, traveled the road from an uptight, bundle-of-nervous-energy perfectionist and mother of four lively children to a calm (most of the time), collected (usually), active businesswoman and church and community volunteer—all the while balancing my outside life with personal needs and those of my family.

True, I am not riding a totally smooth superhighway. I have not fully "arrived." Occasionally I hit bumps and detours in the road. But pressure is rare, and my general level of satisfaction is high. The process is a journey, and I am well along the road.

You can get there too. In this book I show what has brought me—and others—to this point.

Be assured that this journey is also what God wants for you. The angels heralding Jesus' birth joyously sang out, "Peace on earth . . ." Jesus himself said, "Let not your hearts be troubled . . . My peace I give to you." Peace is one of the nine "fruits" or gifts of the Holy Spirit promised Christ's

3

followers in Galatians, chapter five. Obviously God does not want us to live frantic lives.

Bear in mind that the ideas presented here are options. What works for one person may not work for another. Try those that appeal to you. Find what helps you. Even one concept that works for you will make your life that much richer and more enjoyable.

I hope you find many.

In keeping with the spirit of this book, you'll find that the chapters are short and their messages concise.

2

Realize the Most from Your Life

A Morning Resolve

This day, Lord, is Thy gift of grace,
Wherein I may discern Thy face!
The sunbeams quivering on a tree
Reveal Thy constant care for me;
This glad, green earth, the blue above,
May tell the wonders of Thy love.
But oh, dear Lord, lest blind my eyes
Should grow to Thy wide-lifting skies,
To all Thy gifts of earth and sea,
Lord, keep Thy loving hand on me;
Lest as I journey on my way
I miss the glories of each day!
                    ——Ralph Spaulding Cushman

This is *your* life. It is the only one you will ever have. If you let it get by you, you will not have a chance to live it again. So first of all, if you would enjoy life to the fullest, decide now to make the most of it.

Isn't this self-evident? Don't we already do so? No. Most of us live for "a better day"—tomorrow! In the meantime *today* gets away from us.

Make today count. Notice the rainbows. Smell the fresh flowers. Listen to the changing tunes and tempos of life as you walk through it.

The fun of life comes in traveling it, not in arriving at the destination. Have you ever built a house or bought and redecorated one to your own tastes? You plan and replan for months on end. Then, when you finally get what you want, the thrill is over. It's nice to have, but you find you need a new project. The greatest satisfaction came in the process of acquiring, not in the possessing.

God also wants you to make the most of your life. St. Paul advised the people in the Ephesian church, "Be careful then how you live, not as unwise people but as wise, making the most of the time" (Ephesians 5:15-16).

You may ask, "Isn't it selfish of me to want to make the most of my own life when other people are dependent on me?" No. The truth is just the opposite. When you are joyful, your joy reflects like a mirror onto those around you. Enthusiasm spreads like wildfire, wherever it finds receptive timber. Smile at the world, and it smiles back at you. Stare at it grimly, and people wearily turn their heads away.

Find Your God-given Role

Each of us is called to live as the Lord leads and directs us. The biblical Jeremiah, David, and Paul believed that God had a destiny for their lives, preset before they were even born (Jeremiah 1:5; Psalm 139:15-16; Galatians 1:15). However, they didn't know what it was until it unfolded.

You, too, have a God-given role in the ongoing drama that is your life. Only God knows what that is. If you ask, God will unfold it for you as you move along.

Just knowing that is, in itself, a great stress-reliever. I remember vividly the life-changing day that I came to realize I was going to live as long as, and not a moment more or less than, God had in mind for me. Similarly, each day I will

6

accomplish as much as, but no more than is needed, to do what God wants from me that day. On frantic days, I tell myself, *Calm down. If something doesn't get done today, it will get done if and when God wants it done.* That thought immediately relaxes me and enables me to enjoy what comes, as it comes, knowing that if a goal is not accomplished that day, I need not fret. It wasn't meant to happen.

Carrying out your life role is an individual responsibility. No one else can do it for you. Your life may revolve around your family and may involve a lot of other people, but only you can know and do what is right for you in any and every given situation. What works for you may differ dramatically from what works for someone else. My family potlucks our holiday dinners, which have numbered at times as many as twenty-two people. I have a large dining table with four leaves, and I love the fellowship, the noise, and the crowd. A sedate friend of mine prefers to entertain her horde one family at a time in a local restaurant.

Use Time Wisely

Make the most of your time. Discriminate. Avoid unnecessary time and energy wasters. Say no to do-nothing meetings, time-wasting projects, and unimportant events. We humans are slow to drop traditional and familiar practices. Churches were installing church-supper-sized kitchens long after potlucks became the "in" thing. Most group leaders schedule meetings monthly, whether they are needed or not. Two hours spent making name tags or table favors for a church supper may be a time-consuming project you can't afford.

Learn to say no. Your time is precious. Ask yourself, Where is it needed most? Best-selling author Richard Foster claims in *Freedom of Simplicity* that we need to abandon what others say and think. Act on your own priorities, not what you think is expected of you. You may be delightfully surprised to find that others respect your decision to say no. Those who don't may just be envious. But whether they are or not, those persons who don't want to accept your right to say no don't have *your* interests at heart.

You know what you can and cannot do. As God's servant in the world, you need to work out with God what your life should include. Follow that path without concern for hurting other people's feelings over solicitations they make of you.

When you say no, don't explain why. Some people will take advantage of that and try to argue with you over what is in essence your decision and yours alone. You do not owe others an explanation for turning down a request—only courtesy and graciousness. "No," or "No, thank you," or "No, thanks— that's not for me" are good ways to reply. I especially like this one: "I am not comfortable with that." No one can take exception to or argue with any of these responses.

The uneasiness you may feel in saying no may be due to unearned guilt. You want to do your share. You worry that others may be burdened if you don't. To ease your mind, remember that God expects of you only what you can comfortably accomplish. Recall your priorities. And recognize that it is other people's responsibility also to say no when they need to. You are not responsible for their anguish if they do not.

Make Your Own Choices

Express your individuality. Don't let fads, fashions, traditions, or other people's ideas or values determine what you do. Fashionable styles and colors change at the whim of designers. Not every style looks good on your body frame or suits your temperament and taste. Following fashion in clothing or home decor should be a decision you make because the item is something you want, because what you have is wearing out, or because you are tired of your belongings and like the current merchandise, not just because there is a new style.

I decided some years ago not to get my ears pierced. I didn't want to be encumbered with keeping the holes open. Also, I didn't want to have to buy earrings for every outfit (I'm a fanatic about matching apparel). And, I don't like the look of pierced ears without earrings.

Today's selection of earrings for persons without pierced

ears has become limited, but I have no regrets. On the other hand, I like to wear eye makeup. I like the look. Many of my friends with pierced ears don't want to bother with eye makeup. To me it is worth it.

What other people think doesn't matter when it comes to taste. Taste is an individual thing. Follow your own preferences. Honor the selections others make, and expect them to honor yours. It is the differences between us that make human beings so interesting.

Be Willing to Change

Last year my family of four adult children and their families dropped the traditional gift exchange at our family Christmas party. It was my idea. I had several reasons. Our families already buy what we need when we need it. It is hard for all of us to find time to shop at that hectic time of the year. But most importantly, the commercialization of gift-giving has gradually been diminishing the true spirit of Christmas for me. I have found myself neglecting more and more the real reason for celebrating the day. In recent years I have spent far more time shopping, wrapping, and exchanging gifts than singing, worshiping, and praising the Christ child.

One of my daughters relished the idea of not exchanging gifts and proposed that we give each other gifts any time of the year *except* when they are expected. That way they are truly gifts, she says. In place of our dropped tradition she decided to "adopt" a poor family for the holiday. A second daughter living out-of-town was greatly relieved. Her free time is rare, and she finds shopping decisions difficult because she does not see us often.

A third daughter did not welcome the idea, however. She highly values our traditional Christmas Day get-together because she is a single parent and has no in-law family to share the holiday with. To accommodate these differing needs, my husband and I planned separate individual Christmases with each family and had the whole gang over for a post-Christmas Day family get-together. Though we did things differently with each family, this arrangement appears to have worked

9

well, satisfying everyone. I don't know if the change will become permanent. But even if it doesn't, at least we tried to improve a situation we didn't wholly like, and some very good things came from it. It is stressful to go against the societal grain at first, but it is worth it if it satisfies those involved, frees up time, and lightens burdens.

Be Willing to Risk

We Christians especially are so fearful of hurting others' feelings that we miss many opportunities to make a friend, be a friend, or reach out. Don't hesitate to offer help because you may say or do the wrong thing. Say it. Do it. If your words or actions offend, apologize. At least you tried. Most of all, you didn't let an opportunity for friendship or kindness pass you by.

I am not condoning loose or careless speech. Zip the lip if gossip or sarcasm are on your tongue. I am referring to good faith hesitation that is based on shyness, awkwardness, or fear of embarrassment. Go ahead! Embarrass yourself! Then laugh. People are drawn to those in society who can accept their own mistakes and handle them with humor. We love it when people are fully honest and at the same time fully human.

Risk big, if and when the opportunity arises. My husband Peter and I heard several years ago about a recreational vehicle tour through the heart of Mexico. Over a period of forty days, travelers drive through big towns, small villages, and much countryside. The itinerary includes excursions to several Mayan ruins, which have long intrigued me. Cancun was on the trip ticket, as were San Christobel de las Casas, site of the Indian uprising of January 1994, and Mexico City, the world's largest metropolis.

A married couple from our RV club led several of these tours. By the time we became interested, Ken and Carol had gained the experience and competence necessary to handle any problems and emergencies one might run into in an emerging Third World country, foreign in language and culture. Calm, composed Ken had proven himself well able to mold a caravan of strangers into an amiable working group. So Peter and I decided that if the two of them ever escorted a Yucatan tour again when we had the time and money, we would go.

One recent winter it all came together. We were thrilled at the prospect, but I was fearful. I was still recovering from back surgery, unable to ride in a moving vehicle for long periods of time without considerable discomfort. My mother died a few days after we learned about the tour, and I knew the stress of grieving might aggravate my back problem. Then, a few weeks before our scheduled departure, I came down with a virulent strain of the flu, with throat complications that annihilated my voice for three weeks.

I took antibiotics, but they didn't knock out the symptoms. I was still struggling to recover the day we were to leave. Skeptical of Mexican medical facilities, I could easily have bowed out of the trip at that point without feeling guilty or embarrassed. Instead I decided to risk it.

My voice returned the day after we left. Because we rarely traveled far in one day and stopped often, my back handled the trip nicely. As a result, Peter and I experienced a fantastic, once-in-a-lifetime adventure.

Life comes around only once. If we don't get on the train when it pulls into the station, we may never have another chance to ride it.

Above all, be willing to risk a change of jobs, if it will make your life happier. "Now" is what is important. Do you really want to continue typing all day when your heart is set on sales? If you want more time with the kids, why not try working the "graveyard" shift?

Cherish Close Relationships

The greatest joys and deepest sorrows we experience in life are intricately bound up in our relationships with the people we live, work, and spend our leisure time with. Baptismal celebrations, First Communion parties, confirmations, graduations, weddings, and funerals are special times we want to share with those we love. Arguments with spouses

11

and battles with our children grieve us and cloud our ability to maintain our composure, function at top level, and enjoy life fully.

Relationships are living things. They must be nurtured, or they will wither and die. In subsequent chapters we will look closely at ways to strengthen our bonds with family and friends and to resolve conflicts lovingly.

To make the most of your own life and time, avoid taking on other people's problems. You are not responsible for reconciling your feuding brothers. You are not responsible for cleaning up after your teenager. You are not even responsible for taking your children's lunches to school when they are forgotten, though you may want to, depending on the age and circumstances.

Sometimes it is hard to say no in these kinds of situations, but it is best for all concerned when you do. If you bail other people out, they do not learn life's important lessons. Your feuding brothers need to learn how to work things out with each other. Your children need to acquire the habit of taking responsibility for themselves. Be there to support the children, but let them make their own decisions and learn how to cope with occasional failure.

Saying no also avoids hassles over misplaced anger. Those feuding brothers could end up angry at you for interfering, though you were only trying to help. Your children might take out their frustrations over their own negligence on you.

Learn to differentiate between your own and other people's problems and to say no to theirs. It saves you burdens, and it's best for all around.

3

Live Light and Easy

Barbara Brown Taylor relates the story of a man named Ralph who was meeting someone at the airport. As the two men headed toward the baggage-claim area, Ralph kept disappearing—once to help an elderly woman with her suitcase, another time to lift two toddlers to see Santa Claus, and a third time to give someone directions.

"Where did you learn to live like that?" the traveler asked.

"During the Vietnam war, my job was to clear minefields. I saw several of my buddies meet untimely deaths, one after another, right before my eyes. I learned to live between steps. I never knew whether the next one would be my last, so I had to get everything I could out of that moment."

A lighthearted posture and a no-nonsense approach to life go a long way toward freeing up our minds, hearts, lives, and time. Ralph learned early how to live free.

Learn, like Ralph, to live in the moment. Cultivate a continuous mindset in which you take in what is happening around you as it is happening. Watch the people in the cars next to yours at stoplights. Take in the changing greens of the tree leaves as the growing season advances. Look for patterns in the clouds on a cloudy day. It will take some time and effort, but you can acquire this habit of continual awareness.

When you live in the moment, yesterday's troubles and even the hurry-scurry of morning breakfast are left behind. Worries about the future—how you will get the day's work out on time or whether your struggling son will pass his math class—are not allowed to enter. *Now* is all that counts. *Now* gets your full attention.

It is a great way—the only way—to live. We cannot undo yesterday's mistakes. We cannot handle the challenges of the future until they present themselves. If we try to take on these things before they arrive, we waste time and energy. Perhaps even more important, we are letting things we cannot do anything about rob us of our enjoyment of the moment. Isn't that silly? We all do it, of course, but the more we learn to live in the moment, the more we improve the quality of our lives.

Living in the moment is also a great stress reducer. Because we cannot do anything about the past or future, dwelling on them creates an inner tension with no escape valve. Letting go and living in the *now* frees our emotional energies for more constructive use as the day goes by.

Conquer the "Hurry Habit"

Elizabeth Berg, writing in *Woman's Day*, tells how, while shopping one day, she found high-tech frosting that could be spread on cakes *before they cool*. That same night, at her daughter's school open house, the band gave a musical presentation—after the music director cautiously reassured the parents it would take "no more than two minutes."

"This sense of hurry is the norm now," Berg concludes, confessing that she got caught up in it too. Don't we all? But, she adds, "It's not natural." Berg decided to get out of the express lane. "Next time . . . I'll make brownies from scratch, and I'll sit the whole ten minutes that cooling takes, doing nothing but enjoying the smell."

Seek your happiness in simple things. Too often we humans allow the commonplace, the familiar, to become has-beens in our lives. We don't have to do that. Just as we heighten our awareness by living in the moment, we can expand the horizons of our joy by taking pleasure in readily available but nonroutine types of activities. An ice-cream cone on a hot day after work is simple pleasure. A walk around the block on a cold sunny winter day stimulates. A drive out into the countryside clears cobwebs from the brain. Picking raspberries in season gets us outdoors while it brings special culinary delight.

Expand your sense of wonder to bring enchantment to the ordinary. Study a snowflake under a magnifying glass or play with sand, both wet and dry, to bring yourself in touch with God's wonderful world of nature. All that God created is both mysterious and complex. The people God created differ as greatly from one another and are as interesting as are those snowflakes.

Joy often comes in small packages. One recent summer evening two neighbor girls aged nine and twelve were dancing up and down the sidewalk in front of my house. Plumber's plungers in hand (their father is a plumber), they were singing away merrily, "Ah-wee-mah-way," laughing until they doubled over. Up and down the block they went. With each pass they got a little sillier. "They couldn't have more fun at a theme park," I told my husband as we watched through the living room window, as delighted as they were. Fun—even silly fun—is contagious.

Organize and Prioritize

To de-stress your lifestyle, organize and prioritize your time. Organizing eliminates wasted effort and enables you to get more done. Prioritizing cuts out of your life those things that are less important, so that after the "musts," you are doing the things you want and enjoy doing the most. Organize your day and week, especially during the holiday season when things get busier than ever. Later chapters will suggest how.

Plan your life. Where do you want to be at the end of your days? What do you want to have accomplished? What will it take to get you there?

Write down and prioritize the goals that emerge from your plan. Focus on the goal that is dearest to your heart, and lay out the steps required to see it through. Then get started on it.

If you don't start *now* doing what is important to you, you will never get around to it. It will diminish in importance every time you put it off. We have all said at one time or another, "Someday I'm going to... ." Rarely do we go further. When was the last time *you* said that? Did you ever get around to doing it? If not, ask yourself: Is it a significant goal? If so, put it on your list and prioritize it.

Some of you will say at this point—whoa! I thought this book was about slowing down and relaxing. Isn't there a contradiction between being well-organized and living a tranquil life? No. Just the opposite is true. When you have much to do, frittering away your day is what renders it frantic. Good planning prevents chaos and allows more time for restful leisure.

In a commencement speech, University of Wisconsin academic affairs administrator David J. Ward suggested a solution for the time-squeeze lifestyle facing today's graduates: "Work smarter rather than longer." Part of that, he says, is, "Value play."

Plan and prioritize by day, week, and year. Give yourself a little leeway for the unexpected. Modify your plans, if necessary. What you can't do this year, you may have time for next. If you have to wait on some things until the children have left home, that's okay. If you are not a planner, at least try your best to identify your life goals and stay focused on them.

Take Life as It Comes

In any case, take life as it comes. Let things go if they are not working out or working as planned. If you never get around to some of your goals—well, perhaps they just weren't that important to begin with. Perhaps they were not in God's plan for you. Having planned and prioritized, you know you have done your best to achieve what you wanted to accomplish most. It is easier to live with unfulfilled aspirations if you recognize they are of lesser importance. It is easier to live with faded dreams if you know you have done the best you could under the circumstances life presented you.

Of course you should limit your goals to those that are reasonably obtainable. If you are tone deaf but love to sing, don't plan on enhancing the church choir. Instead, confine your involvement to the annual Christmas carol sing for area shut-ins, where hearty participation and love for the Lord are all that matter. If your goal is to become company president, look at the education, skills, and experience needed to get you there; the time and sacrifices you will have to make; and your company's and the industry's attitude toward having women in top management positions. Living light and easy does not require that you restrict your goals to lightweight challenges, but it does require that you choose those you can readily accomplish while retaining comfortable balance in the rest of your life.

We live in a troubled world. Despite all of our own actions to lighten up and enjoy life to the fullest, stressful thunderclouds shadow our lives from time to time. Crises—financial reverses, job losses, the death of a loved one, or serious illness—strike. Or unwanted intrusions come along. A prankster phones you with an obscene message, or a burglar violates the privacy and security of your home.

Life being what it is, expect that the unexpected and unwanted may come your way. We may not want these kinds of things to happen, but they could and sometimes do. Take reasonable precautions. Carry insurance and lock your home. If the worst happens, handle the difficulty with as much grace as you can muster until time heals the wounds.

Two great challenges arise concerning these thunderclouds. One is anxiety. Decide that you will not live in fear of every eventuality. To be constantly in fear is a miserable way to live. You can decide you will not follow that path.

The other great challenge is living with the fallout if such an eventuality occurs. Traumatic events scar our lives. We cannot prevent that from happening. Once burnt by a fire, we hesitate to go near *any* fire again, at least for a time. But we can decide not to become permanently fearful or bitter. We can rest in God's assurance that "All things work together for good for those who love God" (Romans 8:28).

Have Fun

Enjoy work. Work turns the wheels of living. Work is constructive activity, whether that "work" be raising your children, taking the dishes out of the dishwasher, typing insurance forms for the company you work for, or calling a corporate board meeting. Adam and Eve were created for work, to be the caretakers of the world that God had made. "Occupation was one of the pleasures of Paradise, and we cannot be happy without it," said Anna Brownell Jameson. Solomon, noted for his wisdom, says, "There is nothing better for mortals than to eat and drink, and find enjoyment in their toil" (Ecclesiastes 2:24).

Work got bad press after the Fall into sin. It becomes drudgery when we have tasks to perform that we would rather not. But the drudgery mindset is unfortunate and misguided. Working is good for us. In fact, doctors often prescribe it for persons struggling to overcome personal, medical, or emotional problems.

We can decide to enjoy whatever it is that we have to do. Brother Lawrence in *The Practice of the Presence of God* tells how he came to enjoy his dreaded kitchen work by doing it simply and solely for the love of God. Johann Wolfgang von Goethe said, "It is not doing the thing which we like to do, but liking the thing which we have to do, that makes life blessed."

One of the best ways we can live our lives well is to seize joy. Do something just for fun every day. Engage in horseplay with one of your children. Go to lunch with a dear friend with whom you share much. If married, tease your husband with a silly note on his plate at the dinner table.

To live a de-stressed life it's essential for you to find fun within yourself. What do you enjoy doing the most? singing? decorating T-shirts? reading? writing poetry? Does soaking in a bubble bath make you feel like a queen? Then go for it! Pamper yourself. Not at the expense of others, of course, but everyone needs a bit of free time each day. Use yours just for fun.

The busier you are, the more you need it.

Find fun within yourself by learning to laugh at your own frailties. If you cannot do that, you need a crash course in self-esteem. God loves you just the way you are. God was laughing when you absent-mindedly left your own suitcase at home in the flurry and confusion of packing the kids and their assorted paraphernalia into the car for summer vacation. God laughed the day you buttoned your blouse wrong and didn't notice it until you got home from work. God even laughed when you pinched your finger in the storm door and broke it. He knew you would survive and someday come to laugh about it.

Laugh often—at least once a day. Laughing shrinks problems to their true level of ordinariness. If you can't find anything else to laugh at, laugh at your own obstinate, sober-sided seriousness.

4

Make Inner Peace a Daily Habit

*"Only a spiritual man can remove from himself
the tensions that inhibit his relaxation. Then he has
the energy to meet any challenge."*
  ——Branch Rickey, owner of the St. Louis Cardinals

The best way to lighten your life is to start, live out, and
end your day with the Lord. Most of my own personal stress
reduction comes from nothing more than this: choosing daily
to undergird my life with spiritual support. I find strength
and tranquility steadily, even in the midst of hectic, difficult
days, by allowing God to lead me through the day.

I am not alone. One of the most admired women of the
twentieth century was the late Rose Kennedy, mother of our
assassinated president. Rose actively campaigned for the
several members of her family who ran for public office. She
faced numerous hardships and tragedies during her long life,
including the deaths of several of her children, public scan-
dals, the institutionalizing of a mentally retarded daughter,
and her husband's infidelity.

Rose's remarkable character of sweet gentleness blended

with tempered steel was launched in her youth by a lonely stint in a convent. During that time she said she "was able to find in myself the place that was meant for God." For the rest of her life her faith sustained her, and she attended daily Mass as long as her health permitted.

It's true, as the Bible says: "Thou dost keep him in perfect peace, whose mind is stayed on thee" (Isaiah 26:3, RSV).

The spiritual orientation to daily living is freeing. Marcus Borg, professor of religion and culture at Oregon State University, says, "I deliberately try to remember to pray, addressing God as *You* several times each day. On those days I do this, I find more peace and am less burdened by my work. But I'm also much more able to be present to the tasks and people around me. I'm glad to be alive, not burdened with the heaviness that so often weigh us down."

The God-related day makes a vast difference in soothing the hectic pace we often find ourselves getting into. As we put our trust in God, we are mentally putting ourselves into God's time frame instead of living in our own. In God's time frame, it is natural to take life as it comes. This is not true if we slack off instead of making the effort to do our best, however. God expects us to work at honest labor—to do our tasks cheerfully and diligently. The de-stressor is that God expects of us no more than what our capabilities, time, and opportunity allow.

The God-related day also calms the anxieties eating away at us that result from the troubled world in which we live. The end of the cold war brought relief in one arena—fear of nuclear holocaust—but the satellite nations that arose from the breakup of the Soviet Union are extremely unstable, as are the many small nations harboring terrorist weapons. Other fears remain—fear of pollution, overpopulation, and resource depletion. And the list of anxieties has grown to include the proliferation of gangs with guns, frightening statistics on violence and crime, an alarming divorce rate, and increasing stories of sexual abuse and of corruption in business and government. There is no doubt about it; our society is not as comfortable or as safe as it was a few decades ago or as we would like it to be.

When we put ourselves in God's care, however, fears subside. We begin to recognize that we are all part of something bigger than ourselves—God's world. God is in charge. Though he gives all human beings the freedom to make their own decisions and to "do their own thing," from behind the stage curtain God really runs the show. "Be still, and know that I am God!" says Psalm 46:10, affirming that God has final control over what is going on in world. We are promised in Psalm 91:11 that, "He will command his angels . . . to guard you in all your ways."

There is an invisible spiritual world surrounding us that many of today's empirical, scientific minds cannot prove and therefore find hard to accept. Those of us who have been there readily attest to its reality and its power. It is great to have a heavenly Father as a full-time ready adviser and helper for every need. The Bible validates this presence of a loving Creator in Numbers 9:15-23, where the Lord was visibly present with the Israelite people, providing for this huge mass of people moment by moment for forty years while they journeyed through harsh, forbidding desert country.

God can and will take care of us at all times and in all situations today. Just as God has a plan for each of us as individuals, he has a plan for the whole world. And God will see it through. The reason things often look bleak is that God's plan often involves letting people experience the consequences of godless behavior. Sometimes, for God's followers, it is because he has a special plan in mind for us.

A deep level of spirituality comes hard for most people in our modern culture. We are encouraged from little on to take responsibility for and to depend on ourselves. As a result, we miss out on the greatest source of strength, energy, and power available to us. If you are skeptical about the changes the God-related life can make, try leaning on God for a few weeks—bit by bit, if not all at once. If you try this with an open mind and heart, it will change your spirit, your heart, your mind, and your life.

To Bring God into Your Day . . .

Start each day with some early morning personal time with God. Find a five- to ten-minute chunk of time, and turn this time mentally over to God. Read, pray, or meditate until you feel calm and collected, ready to face the day with tranquility. I use a selected group of readings from *The Pocket Prayer Book* compiled by the United Methodist bishop, Ralph Spaulding Cushman. I especially like this one, written by Bishop Vincent:

> I will try this day to live a simple, sincere and serene life, repelling promptly every thought of discontent, anxiety, discouragement, impurity and self-seeking; cultivating cheerfulness, magnanimity, charity, and the habit of holy silence; exercising economy in expenditure, generosity in giving, carefulness in conversation, diligence in appointed service, fidelity to every trust, and a childlike faith in God.

Find the time that works out best for you. Can't find any? Then get up a little earlier, before anyone else is up. If doing this is initially a sacrificial burden, don't lose heart. It will quickly become a joy-filled, peaceful time that sets a more leisurely pace for your day and soon develops into a treasured part of it. If you try it for thirty days, you will never give it up.

What about those people who have to deal with traumatic life problems such as the loss of a limb or the death of a child? How can simple prayer help such people to serenity? In surprising ways.

A number of years ago I was plagued with daily head and neck pain from deteriorating cervical disks. On a few occasions I felt so much pain upon awakening that I didn't want to move, much less get out of bed. Pain is a depressant, creating feelings of hopelessness. I wondered on such mornings how I would ever get through the day.

On those days, I got in the habit of praying, "Lord, whatever happens today, just be with me and help me through it." Though I did not always get full relief from the pain, I floated through every one of those days as if on a cloud, in a physical/mental state I have come to call "peace in the midst of pain." I couldn't really call them "good" days, but they were serene and surprisingly satisfying.

Are you someone who needs a miracle to get through a problem or a difficult life situation? If so, ask God for your miracle. Give him a chance. There were more than a million Israelites wandering around that desert wilderness those forty years, and they needed a lot of food. God provided it in the form of "manna that fell from the sky like rain," the Bible tells us. Archaeological evidence uncovered in recent years supports their story of a massive trek through the desert. God also gave them water to drink from out of a rock. And, amazingly, their clothes and shoes never wore out during all those desert years (Deuteronomy 8:4).

Even today, followers of God occasionally report miraculous interventions and healings—supernatural visions, cancer remissions, and plane trips missed that turned out to be crashes avoided. God doesn't always provide miracles, of course, but we short-change him if we say he is not actively working his love and will in today's world. Three-and-a-half years after surgery for my neck problem, I was still plagued with frequent, disabling pain that the doctor could not explain. One day, exasperated to the nth degree, I prayed hard for relief. God promised it to me soon after, in the middle of a Sunday worship service. Six months later the pain suddenly, inexplicably subsided.

As the day goes on, put problems as they arise into God's lap. I have found this a hard habit to acquire. I tend to get so preoccupied with the details of my day that I forget. When I do remember, I find it generously rewards the pray-er. With time and practice, the remembering comes more frequently. And the benefits are immediate. I have prayed in the midst of an emotional battle with a rebellious teen and found things suddenly cooling off. I once prayed to get home safely after my aging car's brakes failed as I pulled up to a stoplight. The rest of the way home, they grabbed every time.

End Each Day with Spiritual Peace

Close each day by putting everything that happened that day into God's hands. I find the best time to do this is at bedtime, but any time period at or near the end of the day will do.

During this time, thank the Lord for the blessings of your day. The habit of thankfulness keeps fresh in our minds and hearts the true Source of all of the good things that happen to us. This is not an arbitrary world. Though God does give evil a certain amount of latitude, he wants us to prosper. If our heavenly Father shows caring concern for such lesser forms of life as the lilies of the fields and the birds of the air, Jesus says, wouldn't he be even more providential to those created in his own image, the human beings chosen to be the caretakers of his world?

Sometimes it is amazing what prayer will do. A number of years ago our seven-year-old son Kenny saw pictured on the front page of our local newspaper a young mother with two small children—the family of a Vietnam war prisoner. An adopted boy, he became deeply concerned over these children, whose lives were marred because their Daddy was gone. He began to pray regularly for their father's return. I was a full-blown skeptic. There had been discussions and efforts for many months to return the POWs, all ineffective. But I swallowed hard and said nothing. Good thing! That father was home six months later, much to my amazement as well as that of the rest of the world. This event was unprecedented, for the war was not yet over.

During your evening prayers, confess your sins of the day. Have you hurt someone's feelings? yelled at the kids? blown a responsibility? It has been said, "Confession is good for the soul." The act of confessing relieves a pressure valve—our guilt feelings. Confess by owning up in your mind and to your Lord what you have done wrong.

Confession alone will not give you inner peace. You need to feel forgiven to complete the job. You receive the Lord's forgiveness just by asking for it. It's always there, but we do have to ask for it. We need to do that for our sakes, not for

God's. It's a reminder that we are at all times and in all ways beneficiaries of God's gracious mercy.

Ask forgiveness of the person or persons you have wronged—not with self-flagellation, but with a humble acceptance of your wrongdoing. God does not want us to wipe up the floor with bitter tears. What He wants is for us to admit our guilt with the calm words of concern and the considered action that reveals genuine remorse. To take "considered action," make amends as best you are able.

Don't forget to forgive yourself. That is the hardest part, at least for me. To forgive yourself, you have to swallow your pride. I found this easier when I realized that I was not accepting what Jesus did for me on the cross two thousand years ago until I forgave myself. You'll know you have forgiven yourself if you are no longer dwelling on your past mistakes by rehashing them hours or days later.

One last prayer chore: we need to put our disappointments behind us also. Disappointments usually come from expecting too much of other people, ourselves, God, or all of these. To put them behind you, let go of the expectations that led to your disappointment. Did you really expect your husband would never forget something so important as your birthday? Did you truly believe that your teenager would never rebel on the road to independence? Did you honestly think you would never lose your temper with your troublesome into-everything two-year-old? Put these unreasonable expectations into the fireplace and burn them up. Or drown them in a nearby river. Or place them at the feet of Jesus whose death on the cross forgives all. Do whatever works for you mentally. The trick is to let them go completely.

The cleansing-the-soul process that I have just described enables us to put our problems behind us so that we can sleep peacefully and start each new day without any lingering baggage. Then we can begin again with a clean slate, healthy amounts of resolve, and renewed energy.

5

Make Time Work for You

Pam dreaded getting up mornings. Mondays were particularly bad because Monday meant another tumultuous week lay ahead. One day in desperation she started clocking her daily schedule from rising time to bedtime. Immediately she began to see that she was frequently walking into inevitable time binds. She discussed the problem with her family, and together they made some adjustments. Her time pressures eased and she began to enjoy her daily life more.

There are a number of ways to gain the most and best out of each day without doing mental gymnastics or racing the clock to midnight, as happens in so many families today. Start with the right attitude. Make time work for you instead of being controlled by it.

In his book *Timelock*, Ralph Keyes says that the harder we try to control time, the more it controls us. Are you mentally fighting the clock all day? Decide that you will take control and stay in control of your time. But don't try to "conquer" time. That just increases the pressure. The way to control time is to make it work *for* you.

How Do You Do That?

First, as mentioned earlier, *plan your day* to help you accomplish the most in the least amount of time. Let's face it; you have a lot to do. Letting go and slacking off of your responsibilities may help get rid of the pressure, but you won't feel good about it. The aim of reducing stress is to enjoy life more. Use a daily planner if you find it helpful. However, don't do it if using a planner enslaves you.

Planning your day helps eliminate that biggest of all energy-robbing time wasters—wondering what to do next. Make a list or lists. My family teases me about my mine. I make lists for absolutely everything. One of these days I'm going to have to make a list of all my lists! But they do help me get the job done. Rarely do I forget something that must be taken care of or have to rush out at the last minute to pick up something.

Making lists must work. The first thing my eldest daughter said when I told her I was writing about time management is, "You *are* mentioning list making, aren't you, Mom?" Even my easygoing, laid-back husband has started making lists.

Planning tightens, but it also loosens your day. Making a round trip driving your children to their assorted ballgames and music lessons saves both time and gas. This time can then be used for other important things you want to do.

Use Time Wisely

Pace yourself. Set a comfortable steady stride and then let it ebb and flow. You can't perform at your prime all day or all week or all of the time. Peak performers work in bursts of energy followed by time to loaf, recuperate, and brainstorm before taking on a new task. Corporate business learned decades ago that brief coffee breaks by employees improved the company's overall productivity.

If and when you hit gridlock—being faced with too many things to do at once—tackle the most urgent or important item first. All tasks—even the most worthwhile of achievements—are accomplished one step at a time.

Get in the habit of being ahead of time. Does it take ten minutes to drive to work? Then plan to leave fifteen minutes early. Does it take an hour to drive to Grandma's? Allow an extra ten minutes. Those few extra minutes fly by so fast, you will never know where they went. And, because they are minimal in scope, you will hardly miss them by leaving earlier. But the best reason for being ahead of time is that those precious few moments will feel much longer and more enjoyable because you are relaxed while living them.

Allow plenty of time to accomplish your tasks. Take whatever amount is needed to do what you are doing and do it well. The obstetrician who delivered my third daughter never wore a watch, though he had a huge practice and was head of obstetrics at a large city hospital. Whenever I sat in his office, he looked directly at me, listened carefully, and gave me the time I needed to explain my symptoms and progress. I once asked him why he went watchless. "It just gets in the way of my giving good care," he answered with a smile.

Does your child need you to listen to his troubles with his best friend? Take the time. Does your neighbor and good friend want to talk out her worries about losing her job? Listen to her. This is life—and Christianity—at its richest. Time spent caring never tires us.

Allow extra time. If you think getting your tooth filled in the dentist's office will take fifteen minutes, allow an extra ten minutes in case you have to wait in the reception room or get caught by a slow train at a railroad crossing. If you think it's going to take an hour to do the grocery shopping, allow an hour and fifteen minutes. You might run into a friend you haven't seen for a while and want to chat. Or you may find the shopping takes longer than you planned. The best part is, when you habitually allow extra time, very often you will end up with free time on your hands.

Utilize your free specks of time. Take a small magazine or book of poetry to read in the dentist's office. Keep a pocket prayer book in your purse for anytime you have a spare minute. I keep a little notebook in mine, as do many writers, for jotting down special thoughts and writing ideas as they come along.

Schedule some free time into each day. Free time spent wisely refreshes, restores, and builds energy. You might want to use this time to phone your husband at work in midday and tell him how much you love him. Or to meditate and reflect on some spiritual goal or family challenge for five uninterrupted minutes. Some people might find it invigorating to indulge in some body stretches or a total relaxation exercise. One of the best uses of this time is to take a short nap, if you are lucky enough to have this opportunity. Experts say that twenty minutes at midday is sufficient to completely revitalize the body. Some of the most accomplished persons in history were nappers. Thomas Edison practiced the habit, as did Winston Churchill and Harry Truman.

Whatever you choose, use your free time as it best suits your needs and your frame of mind at the time.

Do your work during your best time, if you have a choice, and take your breaks as you feel they are needed. Writing requires long uninterrupted periods of concentration. I find I accomplish the most by taking a quick five-minute break at midmorning and no less than a thirty-minute lunch hour. I don't work at night or during the wee hours, as many writers do, because I don't produce good material at that time of day. And my weekends are a needed respite. Find *your* best and worst times and work with and around them to the best of your ability.

Interruptions and Time Crunches

Revise and re-pace your day, as needed. Interruptions are frequent visitors. View them not as enemies, but as colorful characters that surprise and enliven your routine. Wouldn't life be boring if we could anticipate and plan for every eventuality? Sometimes, of course, we get too many "surprises" at one time and a little boredom is welcome. But as a general rule, accept delays and diversions as normal, and expect to have to shift with the wind as your day moves along.

If you get bogged down at some point, walk away from your task for a few minutes. Are you frustrated over a disappointing phone call? Did the job you thought was completed develop a kink? Give yourself a chance to regroup. A little distance—just a two-minute change of scene or thought pattern—often restores perspective and energy.

Has your teenager just thrown you a curve? ("I *won't* go to Sunday school! None of my friends do!") You can answer, "We'll talk about this later," and mull over how to address his concern while praying for a good response. Better that than to deny his feelings: "You *will* go and that's that!"

Time crunches are inevitable, of course. This is not a perfect world. We don't always plan well. And those interruptions can really disrupt a schedule.

When those time crunches come along, ask for help from coworkers, or at home from the children and, if married, from your husband. Supermoms don't make good role models. Nobody expects or wants you to overextend yourself, at least not regularly. God doesn't, because we can't do our best work when we are overly tired and out of sorts. In loving relationships, people pitch in and help each other when help is needed. Some of my fondest memories as a parent are of those days when I was sick or had a bad day and my children showered me with concern and helpfulness. Even the toddlers played more quietly on my sick days, sensing somehow that I needed a calmer climate just then.

Most of the time we don't get assistance because we don't ask for it. We don't take the time or trouble. Ask. It's a good habit to get into. And, believe it or not, it will make your family appreciate you all the more. Often children and husbands don't notice when we are getting weary.

Don't wait until you are already tired and cranky to request support. Your family would much rather have a calm, collected mother and wife than one who is grouchy and disagreeable. You'll like yourself better, too, if you get in the habit of asking for help at the beginning of a crunch rather than when it is already getting to you.

Getting help from others promptly whenever it is needed is the ideal scenario. But what if coworkers or other family members are nonexistent, are not there when you need them, or are too tired themselves? Then skip whatever you can. You don't *have* to get the carpet vacuumed tonight, even if it is accumulating a lot of lint and who-knows-what. It can wait another day. If the task is something you can't avoid—supper, for instance—eat out or switch the menu to fix-your-own peanut butter sandwiches or whatever. My children loved Sunday night suppers at our house because at that meal they could prepare whatever they wanted.

If time crunches come along when you have a meeting you must attend, arrive late and apologize. Arriving late is better than getting a speeding ticket or, worse yet, having a car accident. If you are usually ahead of time, people who know you will understand. The others will too, once they know you are generally reliable. If the meeting is a job demand and you *must* arrive on time, work around the crunch and cut time somewhere else.

If time crunches come along frequently, perhaps you need to shift gears and drop something. This is an indication your life is too crammed. Part of good time management is planning no more than what you can as a rule handle well. Look back at your daily or weekly plan or even your life plan. Check your goals again, place them in order of priority, and see what you can eliminate.

Special Problems

Save time at work by controlling your paperwork. The more paper you have to sort through to find wanted information, the longer it takes. What can you safely throw away? If the information is available elsewhere and easy to obtain when you might need it, toss your copy.

Are you compressed in your job by technological pressures? A national magazine article pointed out that "technology is increasing the heartbeat" of today's workers due to the information explosion and the time-shrinking capacity of computers and computerized goods and services. "Time is being eaten up by [our] new inventions," says Robert Shrank, a New York City management consultant, astonished that we now have a supercomputer that operates at a trillionth of a second. A Hollywood publicist says, "The fax line has destroyed any sense of patience . . . People are so crazy now that they call to tell you your fax line is busy."

Recognizing the problem is a giant step toward overcoming

it. Don't get caught in this time trap. If you are already there, slow down. There is only so much data one person can digest. You don't *have* to work at breakneck speed just because your computer does. Decide that you will maintain a steady, manageable pace, put out your best effort, and work serenely. If you cannot do that, think of creative new ways to do your job. Would a different piece of software enable you to do more in less time? Or can you talk your boss into hiring additional help to give you needed support? If not, and if this particular work is affecting your health, can you make a beneficial change to a position that is less stressful and more pleasurable?

Modern technology also creates stress. We have become so dependent on such things as electricity, automobiles, and computers that when they cease to function, we are put out of business and cannot get our work done. To counteract this dilemma and the stress it creates, put backup systems in place to cover your areas of greatest need.

In our personal lives, television compresses time. To hold viewer interest, camera operators change the shots every six seconds or so by closing in on or backing away from the subject, changing the camera angle, or redirecting the action to a second camera. This frequent shifting has shortened the attention spans of children. What does it do to adults who watch television frequently? In the late '70s MTV exploded on the scene with constant bursts of changing images. The hectic impact of this frequent change of motion has to rub off on our psyches. Be aware of how it affects you.

Many people allow television to control their time by scheduling their evening hours around their favorite programs. If you are pressed for time and see yourself in this picture, make life easier for yourself. Change your viewing habits. Decide to turn off the set at a certain hour. If a highly desired show is coming up, videotape it for watching later.

Use technology aids. Some people today find shopping on-line and electronic banking time-saving. But make certain the technology you use is helpful. Technology can also waste time. Some kitchen gadgets are not worth getting out of the cupboard, because of the time lost cleaning them. Computers, for all their marvelous accomplishments, do not necessarily make small tasks easier. It is quicker and simpler to write up a new recipe by hand than to boot up the system to make an entry. Most computer users find they can balance the family checkbook and budget faster by hand.

Time Management Helps

Prompt decision making is important to good time management. When faced with a choice, look at once at all of the factors involved, choose the best option you see, and act on it. If you feel you must give extra time to an important decision, mentally put it on a shelf and let it rest a while. Our subconscious can work wonders solving problems while we are actively engaged in other activities. This is true with decisions we must make jointly as well as individual ones.

Don't take *too much time* to make your decisions. Kathleen Eisenhardt, associate professor of strategy and organization at Stanford University, studied fast and slow decision-making in twelve Silicon Valley companies. The fast deciders took two to four months to make a major decision, such as introducing a new product line. A slower group took up to eighteen months. Surprisingly, the findings showed that the faster group collected more data, considered more alternatives, and worked through their options more vigorously than did the slower group. They stayed focused. The latter, in trying to gather every last bit of information and reach one hundred percent agreement, lost sight of the bigger picture and got bogged down.

Taking action expeditiously also saves time. Procrastination is wearisome. Think about it. When you know you have to get a letter off to your mother and you keep putting it off, it churns in your mind, consuming empty time and limiting capacity to attend to other matters. Suzanne Caygill, a renowned design consultant of celebrities' homes and wardrobes, followed a rule she learned from her grandmother: If you have a job to do, get at it immediately. Too many people waste time "commencing to proceed to get started."

Striving for perfection, too, can be counterproductive. Thomas R. Williams, former chairman of Wachovia Corporation, discovered that many young people in banking didn't know when to stop researching a project and start wrapping it up. Writers have the same problem. When do we stop reworking and revising our manuscripts and just send them out? Good time managers recognize when perfection is worth striving for, and when to let things go.

Where possible, use the telephone to handle matters instead of driving or writing a letter. The phone is an amazing time-saver. So are answering machines. If you can't reach your party, leave a message telling the person when you will be available to take their return call. This technique has saved me many repeat phone calls to busy editors or those temporarily out of their office. It saves money as well.

Similarly, schedule your activities to avoid long lines and traffic jams whenever possible. Go to the restaurant early, before the crowds arrive. Shop for groceries over the dinner hour. Don't cash checks on Friday afternoons. Go to work early or stay late, when the phones aren't ringing and there are fewer people around to interrupt you.

If long commutes are robbing you of precious hours each day, use this time productively—to read the newspaper or listen to an important tape, for instance. Those who find commuting a serious, uncorrectable problem may want to find a job closer to home, or move closer to work.

Most of all, stay focused on your goal. Make time work for you, but not so that you can drive yourself to get more and more done. Make time work for you in order to enjoy life more.

Quiz

How well are you doing with your time management? Circle the appropriate reply.

____ I plan ahead (often   sometimes   seldom   never).

____ I waste (little   some   lots) of time.

____ I make decisions (promptly   in good time
with difficulty).

____ I (do   do not) prioritize my activities so that the most important things get done.

____ When interruptions come, I shift gears (easily   with difficulty).

____ When overloaded, I find it (easy   difficult) to ask for help.

____ I (seldom   sometimes   too often) feel hurried during the day.

____ I (often   rarely   never) find free time.

____ I (do   do not) enjoy the usual pace of my days.

6

Is Your Workload Too Heavy?

Diane became increasingly stressed from trying to juggle her home, family, nursing job, and church work. Then her teenage daughter began having problems. So she gave up her job. The break gave her some blessed relief, she said, and a chance to talk more with her daughter. But then her employer, always short of qualified nurses, asked her to come back. She hesitated. If she said no, she might not get a chance to work there again. Her family could use the money, with college costs looming on the horizon. Mostly, she dreaded getting back on a high-stress track. What should she do?

A national magazine article on time pressures attributed almost every reason for running out of time to women working full-time at paying jobs. The article was directed at employed persons, but many women who are not employed outside the home get so caught up in the care of preschoolers, in household tasks, and in church and charity work that they also become stressed out. Almost all women today are overburdened to some extent by the demands made of them in their home and family lives.

Obviously we cannot even consider lightening our lives without looking hard and long at overly heavy workloads as a primary source of stress. The most difficult role is that of the working single parent. But making the decision to work or not to work is not an option for some, and not an easy decision for others. Also, stress overload does not necessarily arise just from holding down a job.

If you are an over-stressed working woman, determine first of all where the pressure-cooker feeling is coming from. Is it from problems on the job? from not having enough time for everything? or both? If your first response is job-related problems, address these first.

Job-related or General Superstress?

The last chapter covered some forms of job stress, but there are others. Jobs are so tenuous today that almost all employees feel somewhat enslaved to the demands of their work. Those in executive positions experience added stress; there is a higher sense of responsibility and commitment at upper levels, and the competition to get and keep your job is keener.

Some career women succumb to "climbing the ladder" madness: Success is the goal, and whatever it takes to get there is the price you have to pay. The temptation to break the glass ceiling is savory and sweet, now that it is attainable for many women. "You get addicted to overworking," one professional woman said, citing her experience as a partner in an insurance firm.

More women are becoming workaholics. Does your job or career dominate your life so much that your health, marriage, and family life are suffering? If so, you are at risk. This does not mean that you must give up your job; but you do need to pause, step back, and look at what's happening. Are you climbing the ladder on the wrong wall?

Dr. Herbert Freudenberger, co-author of two books on burnout, advises workaholics to avoid taking on any tasks that are unrelated to their jobs. Workaholics also need to learn to screen their tasks for relative importance. "Tune in to your emotions," he adds, "and make yourself take breaks and an adequate lunch hour."

If, on the other hand, you are a working woman stressed out from extending yourself too far in your overall life, look at your reasons for working, your family situation, and your priorities. Then ask yourself if your job is accomplishing what you want it to. Are you getting what you need and want from it? Is it worth the sacrifices you must make in your personal and family life? Have you considered other options that might work better for you and your family?

Those of you who are contemplating working or are returning to the working world should ask these same questions.

Reasons Women Work

Historically, women entered the work force for a number of reasons. The working women's movement started with World War II and the subsequent advent of labor-saving devices. Women were needed in the factories to help manufacture war products. That got them out of the house and lent respectability to their being in the working world. In the years that followed, automatic washers, wash-and-wear clothes and household fabrics, and automatic dishwashers came on the market at affordable prices and quickly became household essentials.

Women suddenly had extra time on their hands, particularly in the years after their children entered school or left home. Many women went back to college, fulfilling dreams in a world now opening its doors to women's full talents and capabilities. The feminist movement added momentum to this cultural change.

Because the cost of buying a home and raising children was a formidable challenge for the average middle class family, many women went to work simply to ease a tight budget. This trend solidified in the 1970s, when real earnings began to erode for the low and middle classes. In the decades that followed, hourly wages progressively lagged behind inflation, further reducing household purchasing power. The steep increase in the cost of health care and health insurance premiums in the late 1980s and '90s accelerated this plight. Most divorced single parents work because they must in order to support their families.

When women thronged into the work force, they found that

41

a gratifying sense of self-esteem accompanies getting a paycheck. For years women had complained that their work in
the home was undervalued, if not unappreciated. I myself felt
that way. I can still remember my special joy when, after
several years of at-home parenting, I got a job—and a paycheck—teaching in a nursery school. It wasn't the money.
Nursery school teachers do not bring in high salaries, and
the job was part-time. But the income felt great to a woman
whose unpaid workload had revolved for years around the
stove, the washing machine, and diapers.

I believe the problem of homemakers feeling undervalued
is nearly universal, for society has repeatedly made efforts
to glorify the job, and they have all fallen flat. It is hard to
recognize your worth when no money comes in and you see
no progress. As one stay-at-home mom said in a newspaper
documentary on the working mom: "You don't have measur-
ing sticks when you stay home. There aren't true markers
from 5 a.m. to 8:30 p.m. to show that you accomplished
something." An ex-teacher says, "With teaching I felt I had a
grip on how to do new things. But with parenting, I'm never
100 percent sure."

How sad. There is enormous worth in the raising of children and the creating of a healthy, happy home. As William
Ross Wallace once said, "The hand that rocks the cradle is
the hand that rules the world." Unfortunately, society has yet
to find a significant and appropriate way to honor full-time
parenting and homemaking. Although it is not the choice of
all, and not an option for many, the full-time-at-home role
has great value that should be recognized.

Understand Your Reasons for Working

If you are employed, and not of necessity, do you know why
you are working? Focusing on your true motives brings
comfort and peace of mind, if you are comfortable with them.
If you are uneasy about them, knowing that and responding
accordingly may help you find that peace.

Are you working just to keep busy? Many women do. If so,
is your lifestyle choice working out well for you and your

family? If not, did you overlook or minimize how much holding a job might affect your personal and/or family life? This complication doesn't get much press in a world in which the feminist movement endorses so emphatically choosing a career.

If you are working for this reason and have some doubts, ask yourself: Does my working satisfy my goals for myself and my family? What is lacking, and what will it take to remedy that?

One couple claims that following the two-income family lifestyle is not a matter of survival or fulfillment for them. Rather, "It's the way we get extra things. I grew up in a poor family with four kids, and we had no extras. There's no way my kids are going to be like that." Are you working "to get extra things"? Are you happy with the price you must pay to get them, in terms of the quality of your personal and family life?

Many women with professional careers are working for fear they might lose their jobs, their place in the corporate structure, or their investment in their education if they stay home to raise their children. This is a genuine concern. A few friends of mine, professionals with master's degrees who had been in the working world for several years, dropped out to raise their babies from infancy to school age. Both said they knew they would have to take lower-ranked jobs when they returned.

This is an unfortunate reality. Field contact is important. Once you leave a position, you lose the continuity and awareness of what is going on in that field or market. One of my daughters did substitute teaching during her first year out of college instead of getting another kind of full-time job, just so that she could stay in touch with the job openings for music teachers. It paid off. She had a job in her field the following year.

If you are caught in this kind of dilemma, analyze the situation and look at the long-range view. What are your options? Could you pick up your career again later? If you lost your place and had to come back at a lower level or find a job elsewhere, would it be worth it to you? If the outlook still looks out of the question, how about back-stepping to a job share or other part-time position? Or could you act as a consultant, working from your home, to stay up in your field?

What are *your* reasons for working? For some, the income is a necessity. For others it eases the hard edges of life. The self-esteem and sense of fulfillment that jobs and careers bring is important to some women and vital to others.

Are your reasons mixed? Most of the time, ours are. Because we are complex human beings with a large assortment of wants and needs, it is sometimes hard for us to discern the relative importance of things. God gives us varying talents, not all of them in the areas of parenting and homemaking. What is right for one person is not necessarily right for all or for someone else. Each of us must find her role, ideally choosing the one that God wants for her.

Quiz

To help you clarify your reasons and differentiate true needs from wants, check the answers below that most closely resemble your situation. If you wish to focus more closely on your true reasons, give each answer a percentage rating after the response.

1. I work because I (we) need the money or the health care coverage.

    ____ without a doubt

    ____ probably true

    ____ partly true

    ____ not at all

2. I work to get extra things for my family.

    ____ without a doubt

    ____ probably true

    ____ partly true

    ____ not at all

3. I work to keep busy.

____ without a doubt

____ probably true

____ partly true

____ not at all

4. I work for the satisfaction and fulfillment it brings me.

____ without a doubt

____ probably true

____ partly true

____ not at all

5. I need to work to recoup the investment in my education.

____ without a doubt

____ probably true

____ partly true

____ not at all

6. I work because I have an emotional need to hold a job.

____ without a doubt

____ probably true

____ partly true

____ not at all

7. I love my children dearly, but I work because the stress of 24-hour-a-day 7-day-a-week parenting would drive me crazy.

____ without a doubt

____ probably true

____ partly true

____ not at all

Are you comfortable with your reasons for working? If not, take this important matter to the Lord in prayer and seek guidance with an open mind. This way you can be assured peace of heart about your decision, whatever it is.

A number of years ago my husband was given a job opportunity in another state. The transfer would mean leaving our parents and relatives behind to move into a strange new community. The job was in office work rather than sales, which meant less income potential for our family. But it also meant he would no longer have to work nights and Saturdays. I knew without asking that this was God's plan for us, for amazingly just a week before the offer came, Peter had said to me over coffee one morning, "I love my job, but I don't want to do this kind of work all of my life. I want to spend more time with you and the kids."

Volunteer Overload

Overload in your volunteer life generally comes from over-obligating yourself. The obvious solution is to cut back on your commitments. Say no courteously but firmly. God expects only so much of you. The volunteer ranks are thinning since women entered the working world *en masse*. You cannot make up for the slack by yourself.

Volunteerism has to change with the times. Church groups, scout programs, and school committees must do things new ways. My church has several active women's circle groups—a rarity today. My own circle found a good solution for the circle chair position, which nobody wanted to take because of the extra time involved. We use co-chairpersons. If one of the chairwomen can't make the board meeting, the other takes it, and they share the other duties.

If you are stressed by some volunteer task you have taken on, do something about it. If you dislike making phone calls, turn the job over to another member of the committee who doesn't mind telephoning, or simply decline. If your child's soccer team cannot find a coach to replace you, so be it. This is a group problem, and it is the group's responsibility to take care of the matter in whatever way they can. In the final analysis, if God wants the task done, he will provide a person or a way.

7

Determine the Best Role for You

"The pursuit of a simpler life with deeper meaning is a major shift in America's private agenda," *Time* magazine reported in a 1991 article. "There is a sense of enormous trade-off between a fast-track career and family well-being," economist Sylvia Hewlett says. "Women can see the damage all around them and are making different choices than they did a few years ago."

If you are fortunate enough to have the option of choosing whether or not to pursue a job or career, making that decision is nonetheless often difficult. In this chapter we will look at the pros and cons of working and of the stay-at-home life, some factors to consider when making or affirming your decision, and a number of alternate work options for those who wish to work in a lighter or more home-centered type of work role.

Looking at the Work Choice

We've already discussed the benefits of securing paid employment. But working has disadvantages, too. Holding down a job obligates us. We have to show up faithfully because the company depends on us. Women who own their own businesses must work the long hours that satisfy customers, do the essential paperwork, and see that the cleaning chores in the store or office get done.

Working means added expenses for you and your family. You have to pay income and Social Security taxes on your earnings as well as transportation costs to and from work. Career and professional women must subscribe to journals in their fields. Child care is costly if you have little ones or school-age summer vacationers, and finding quality child care is often difficult. With some jobs, you have to enhance your wardrobe and pay costly dry cleaning bills to keep it up. You need to buy your lunch if you don't feel like packing one. Most working women indulge in take-out or restaurant dinners frequently for those evenings when they come home too tired or frazzled to cook. Some find they need a car phone to keep in close touch with their office or the sitter.

Many married couples feel the benefits of mom's working are not worth the net income after all of her expenses are factored in. Years ago I stopped substitute teaching when I realized that my sitter was taking home more than half of my paycheck, and I still had all of my housekeeping to do when I got home. I enjoyed teaching, but it wasn't worth the price I had to pay.

The Stay-at-home Life

It is becoming trendy again for mothers of young children to stay home to raise them. The stay-at-home life has many pluses. The pace of life is slower and easier, though hectic at times when there are lively toddlers around. It feels good to be more in control of your life and your time.

The stay-at-home life brings moms of wee ones great spiritual rewards. One woman, who dropped out of teaching when she became pregnant, said it was not her children's first words or first steps she feared missing; it was the extra acts of love. "Max hugs me six times in a hour," she says. "If he were with someone else, he'd be giving those hugs to someone else."

This mother likes being able to set the behavior standards for her children all day long. Also, she and her husband think she can give her children better care than a day-care worker would because she has a greater emotional investment in them than would a non-family member. For Christians, it is a way to be certain our children are constantly being taught biblical values.

The mother described above also likes being able to keep her three children together rather than seeing them separated as would happen in her day-care facility. A bonding takes place between siblings, one that is strengthened when children stay together. Of course, children are not always separated in day care. Concerned working parents can chose their facility accordingly, if this is important to them. Some children may need it and some may not, depending on their ages and personalities.

The stay-at-home life has drawbacks, too. It is not all sunshine on fields of daisies. One-income families must lower their financial expectations. Mothers who leave the working world find that the initial adjustment is hard and takes time. At-home moms can go for days without talking face-to-face with another adult during the day.

If you are a stay-home mom burdened by the isolation of the lifestyle, take an exercise class or lunch with friends once a week for a few hours. If getting a temporary daytime sitter is impossible, take in activities where you can bring the children along. Make trips to the stores or library (children's section), join a daytime Bible study group that provides nursery service, or enroll in a nursery school that uses mother volunteers. This rewards both mother and children.

Staying home is not for everyone, even among those who are able to make this choice. Not every parent has good parenting skills. Some women lack patience. I encountered one such mother in my nursery school. She was a lovely woman and a caring mother, but one fraught with emotional problems. Some women, coming from dysfunctional family backgrounds, have poor knowledge about what it takes to provide a secure, stable home. Only you can know your own and your family's needs and decide what is right for your situation.

Factors to Consider

When you are making or affirming your decision about whether or not to work, and if so, under what circumstances, consider the following factors:

First, and of greatest consequence, *do you have a choice?* Can you afford to stay home or to choose to work part-time? Many women, especially if they are single parents, cannot. If you are the sole support or must contribute substantially to the support of your family, or if you must work to obtain health insurance coverage, your decision is not hard. You simply have to work.

If you are lucky enough to have a choice, before you arrive at a decision *look at your whole situation from a long-range point of view.* Parenting is a temporary life role. The day is coming when the children will be gone. How will you feel then about the decision you are making now as to whether or not to work? Seeing the long road helps to prevent regrets later.

Answers will differ. Some may want to postpone fulfilling career aspirations or working for extra money until their children are in school all day. Others—especially those whose husbands are in demanding professions or occupations—will want to put off working until the children are grown, or may choose never to seek gainful employment. Still others will choose to work part-time throughout family life years. And still others will hold a full-time job or career throughout, feeling comfortable handling both roles.

Another factor to consider—and this is important—is *What makes you happy?* A happy mom is a more capable mother and wife. Mothers who are unhappy in their situations spread their unhappiness around in one way or another. Your family would rather have you happy.

If work, and especially full-time work, is your choice, *can you balance the many roles in your life*—worker, wife, mother, churchperson, responsible citizen in the community, and individual person with needs of her own—to your and your family's satisfaction? It's a tall order. Many women are doing just that today. But many others are having difficulty handling the stresses of this role.

Those who feel pulled from both ends, yet want to or must work full-time, may find the best way to free up more time with the children is to put off housekeeping demands and/or church and community commitments until the empty nest days arrive. The important thing is to find comfortable balance in your work, personal, and family life during these energy-demanding years and to prioritize what is most important to you and your family. A married couple—both ministers—arrived at a good solution for career/family balance. Together they took a single parish. Each worked "half-time" in the congregation in the area of his or her pastoral strengths.

Another factor you need to look at in making your decision is the *general state of your health and well-being*. If you have medical problems, they are apt to pyramid under the added stress of working. Part-time work might be a better choice for you.

Last but not least, *consider your family's needs and welfare*. Like Diane in an earlier chapter, if a member of your family has special needs, you may find it more satisfying to attend to your loved one's needs for as long as your loved one needs your attention.

In short, in determining the role that is best for you, seek God's guidance, be aware of your own and your family's needs, and look at the long-term ramifications of the choice you make.

Alternate Work Options

If you want to work but need to look at less stressful work options, first analyze what is going on. Ask yourself: Does the pressure I feel lie in my holding any kind of job at all, or is it the result of problems I'm having in my present position or with the company I work for? If the working lifestyle is too heavy a burden, you may be able to find an alternative, satisfying option. Can you get your job workload reduced? Could your husband and children pitch in more at home? Can you hire out the housekeeping or use a laundry service? Don't be tightfisted about the cost; it is a good investment if it protects your health and sense of well-being. Also, in determining whether it is worth it or not, factor in the cost of your not working, should you have to quit your job due to stress-related illness. Burnout is a serious, costly ailment.

If you are unhappy with your present job, boss, or company, take a chance and make a change. "Worthwhile advances are seldom made without taking risks," says W. I. Beveridge. Do so promptly. Job difficulties increase tension and rob us of energies that could be used constructively and enjoyably. In a later chapter we will discuss on-the-job relationship difficulties.

If you are overextended on the job and none of the above options is workable for you, could you downshift? Could you job-share or work on a part-time basis? Could you work for a temporary job service? Can you find a similar position elsewhere that demands fewer hours? Can you try another type of work that would take up less of your time and still give you sufficient income, satisfaction, and fulfillment?

Perhaps you could stay home and still work. Can you perform some functions or execute your job from your home? Could you set up a business in your home? Joanne Cleaver has written a book titled *Work at Home Options* for women with an entrepreneurial spirit who want home-based careers so they can maintain both quantity and quality time with their families.

If your choice is the stay-at-home option, but you wonder in light of the present economic climate whether you can afford to, the picture painted these days by economists is positive, according to Marc Levinson, *Newsweek* business writer. The escalating cost of health insurance premiums in recent years is now leveling off. The availability of jobs, should the family's primary breadwinner get laid off or fired, looks favorable: Computer-literate persons are in demand everywhere in the industrial sector, and the heavy hiring in the service sector is for jobs in the middle rather than lower income range. An option for married couples who want one parent in the home is to have Dad stay home with the babies. This works well if both parents agree and if the father's personality lends itself well to parenting little ones and to giving up temporarily the income and prestige of the working world.

If you want to stay home but can't quite manage it on one income, perhaps you could babysit a few other children. I did this when I found that I was spending almost all of my daytime hours, except for naps, with my preschool-age daughters. Toddlers need full-time supervision for those first few years anyway, so why not devote all of your time to child care?

8

Take Good Care of
Your Body

Michael Fortino, a nationally known time-management
expert, revised his advice after "the frantic '80s" because of
these grim statistics: the average professional spends thirty-
four minutes a month exercising, twenty-two minutes a
month reading for pleasure, four minutes a day conversing
meaningfully with the spouse, and less than eleven days in
a whole year fully relaxed. "Most telling of all," he says, is
this: "The divorce rate is now 61 percent and climbing."
Apparently he believes there is a connection. There may be.

Fortino says quality of life should be our goal. He advocates
striving for balance in eight areas of life: health, family or
community, recreation, intellectual and spiritual pursuits,
goals, dreams, career, and money. He puts health first, with
family or community second. Career and money, once topping
his list, he now puts last.

Fortino is correct when he says health and family concerns
must take precedence over jobs. What is working all about,
if not to enrich your life? That doesn't happen if you are not
feeling well or are functioning poorly in your family life.

Health supersedes family concerns because you cannot be
an understanding wife, if married, and/or a patient, caring
mother if you are ailing or are emotionally or spiritually

distressed. In truth, you cannot do anything well or enjoyably unless your personal needs are taken care of. Jesus said, "Love your neighbor *as yourself.*"

In the public mind, health habits are not exactly a fascinating challenge. The common perception is that they really belong in the category of drudgery—tasks that must unfortunately be attended to. Not so. Nothing affects your state of mind and outlook on life more. Nothing shapes your capabilities, molds your mind, and brings more sunshine into your disposition than radiant health and wholeness. This is as true for very busy employed people as it is for children and leisure-laden retirees. Value your health. Make good health—whole health—your foremost goal. It is not hard. And it is great fun—not just for you but also for those you live with. Everybody enjoys being around people who are radiantly alive, well, and happy. You are your children's role model. Give them an inspiring one.

In this chapter I recommend that you use your body's own abilities and natural means (foods rather than drugs) as much as possible to stay well and healthy. This is not only the simplest, but also the healthiest way to live. Our bodies are remarkably engineered to adapt to change and to heal themselves. When professional expertise is required for guidance, I use appropriate competent sources.

The basic formula for good physical care has been around for a long time: eat right, live right (without vices), exercise, and practice good sleep habits.

Eat Right

Consumers today are overly concerned about dietary health risks. Don't you find it annoying that the experts keep changing the rules on what foods to prefer and which are taboo?

If the experts can't agree, why be unduly concerned? One of the best ways to lighten up is to follow time-proven guidelines, stop worrying over the latest developments, and spend the time and energy saved on your family or other important matters.

The food guide pyramid recommended by nutritionists

today has not changed a great deal from the one taught decades ago. Reduced amounts of protein, especially red meats, and less fat content are the only significant differences. This basic diet calls for a wide variety of delicious, tasty foods for your menus. Eat lots of fruits and vegetables—especially fresh ones, and without those fatty dips and sauces we like to put on them to fancy up the meal. Balance this with plenty of grains and pastas, especially whole grains. Add some protein—the body builder—in the form of meat, poultry, fish, eggs, beans, or cheese. Add milk and dairy products for strong bones and teeth.

Plan menus that are enjoyable. Eating has to be fun, or you won't stay with a healthy diet. A visually appealing dinner plate also is important, so vary the colors and textures of the foods. For maximum enjoyment, make sure the food tastes in each meal complement one another.

Sugary desserts are permissible if not overconsumed. They don't have much food value, but they provide energy and satisfy a sweet tooth. The only real hazard is tooth decay. Coffee and salt are relatively harmless unless you have medical problems or you overindulge.

When purchasing foods, select fresh or prepackaged rather than processed foods, where possible. In cooking, choose broiling over frying. Avoid overeating fatty foods, but don't avoid fat altogether. Fat holds the flavors of foods and gives us satiety value. (It stays in our stomachs longer so that we don't feel hungry so soon.) Moderate your use of fat by purchasing flavorful foods to start with and spark up your recipes by using a variety of herbs and spices.

If you are in good health, have no special needs, and follow this diet, you need not concern yourself with studying nutrition labels, taking vitamins, counting calories, or putting too much food on your plate. Good health and weight control will follow. You can even binge on the forbiddens occasionally. The important thing is to use the food pyramid as a regular guide.

The reason so many people have food-related health problems is that they don't eat right to begin with. Fat-laden fast foods (burgers and fries), rushed meals, cherished high-fat foods, and unhealthy snacking do them in. Or they skip breakfast. Eating breakfast helps you fill in the food groups easily, but it is also important because you metabolize your food better earlier in the day. The preferred meal plan is to eat large breakfasts, moderate lunches, and light suppers.

Yes, you can snack. Just make it a healthy snack. Some tasty ones are popcorn (unbuttered), pretzels, jello, celery and carrot sticks, breadsticks, and all kinds of melons and other fruits. Cheese and nuts are also good snacks and good for you, but watch your daily fat intake closely if you munch on them.

Go ahead and binge once in a while. It feels good. It's fun. Done occasionally, it won't harm you. Diets should never be straitjackets, only general guides. My mother, a diabetic, loved ice cream. Her doctor told her, "Go ahead and have some now and then." Why not? She was already nearing her eighties.

Don't diet unless you know you are excessively overweight or your doctor has suggested it. Dieting is extremely overindulged and is generally a waste of time if not unhealthy for you. "America is the most 'fat phobic' country in the world," says Esther Rothblum, a psychology professor who has done numerous studies on fat discrimination. Most people have a "good weight range"—one in which they feel their best and are the most productive. Find yours, be comfortable with it, and follow the eating pattern that keeps you there.

The Mayo Clinic says there is no exact formula for knowing what weight is most healthy for each individual. Weight tables are helpful, but only to a point. You must also consider your body shape and general health. If you are overweight, where you carry the excess weight is important. Do you resemble more an apple or a pear? "Apples" are at greater risk for developing heart disease, high blood pressure, stroke, and diabetes than "pears." To assess risk, measure your waist and your hips at their fullest point. If your waist is larger, you are at risk. Even then, you may not have to lose weight if you are in general good health. If you are under the charted weight level for your height, again you have nothing to worry about unless your general health is suffering.

If you must lose weight, do so by reducing the fat grams in your diet. This is the best, easiest, and most comfortable way to shed excess pounds. You can eat all you want, so long as you don't overdo on fats (or sugar). For women, the fat gram guideline in the normal diet is 20 to 40 grams per day. (For men, 30 to 60.) Ask your doctor for a fat-gram-counter chart if you need one to assist you. Also vital to the process is exercise, which makes losing weight easier by increasing your body's ability to burn calories.

Exercise Regularly

Exercise benefits us all in several ways. Just as an automobile runs best when the engine is revved up at least once a week, so also speeding up our internal engines regularly helps them to function at peak performance. Exercise energizes us and, surprisingly, makes us less tired. Regular exercise helps thwart heart disease and diabetes and reduces the risk of stroke.

Many people cringe at the idea of exercising because they think it takes lots of time and trouble. Not true. The Mayo Clinic says you benefit from as little as thirty minutes three times a week. You can accumulate the thirty minutes throughout the day, fifteen minutes here and five or ten there. Every other day is preferred over back-to-back sessions with a long break between.

Make exercise fun. Your program should not be grueling, nor should it be hard to work into your schedule. Even moderate amounts help to protect against early death, the Mayo Clinic says. Walking, jogging, and biking fit readily into most people's lifestyles. Many people use radio or tape headphones to add enjoyment to these jaunts, but if you use them, be aware of the danger of reduced hearing in traffic situations. Classes and exercise groups are fun and help you to keep at it; however, using an exercise machine or tailoring an exercise plan into your workday is easier for many. Friends of mine walk to and from work every day—a distance of several miles. Others walk during their lunch hour. My husband and I aquacize in the YMCA pool because it is one more thing we can do together. If you cannot manage a regular exercise plan, even small bits of activity are of some benefit. Try climbing stairs instead of using the elevator, parking the car a short distance from your destination and then walking there, pacing the sidelines while you're watching your child's soccer game, or circling the mall when you shop. Find what works best into your likes and lifestyle.

Get Proper Sleep

Sleep deficits are common today. Good sleep habits improve our health, disposition, energies, and abilities. People who get plenty of sleep learn better, researchers have found.

People differ on their need for sleep. Some function well on only three hours a night. Others are unproductive and irritable if they get fewer than ten. Your personal need, wherever it falls, will stay about the same throughout your life. Find it and honor it, even if you have to give up something important. Your indulgence will more than pay for itself in increased efficiency and a sunnier disposition.

Follow the same sleep pattern nightly. Our bodies have a cyclical daily rhythm. We function best when we work with it. Dr. William Mayo, one of the founders of Mayo Clinic, went to bed at ten o'clock, regardless of circumstances. If the Mayos were entertaining guests, he politely excused himself.

Everyone has a sleepless night now and then. No serious harm is done. But sometimes people have trouble either falling asleep or staying asleep for days or weeks. If you have trouble over a lengthy period of time, seek medical attention. Chronic insomnia not only robs you of a full enjoyable life, but it also makes you more prone to accidents.

If you just need help occasionally to get a good night's sleep, try these tips. Again, what helps one person may not prove helpful to another. Find what works for you.

1. *Avoid caffeine after your evening meal.* You'll find caffeine in colas, tea, and cocoa as well as coffee.

2. *Shun tobacco.* Nicotine can cause shallow sleeping and sleeplessness.

3. *Deal with worries before you retire.* Write them down, pray over them, and then outline some possible solutions before you go to bed.

4. *Determine the amount of sleep you need and honor it.*

5. *Have a healthful bedtime snack* such as a small glass of milk and a cookie. Doctors don't know why, but people sleep better if they are not hungry.

6. *Relax.* Don't work too hard at getting to sleep. Let nature take over. Your body is designed to drift naturally off to sleep. Try reading a book, listening to music, or watching television to get your mind off the fact you're having trouble getting to sleep.

7. *Avoid clock-watching during the night.* Hide your alarm clock, if you tend to watch it.

8. *Reduce the time you spend in bed.* Too much time can cause shallow sleep. Cut your bedtime by an hour or two.

Other Bodily-Care Needs

Years ago, health experts recommended that we get lots of fresh air. Clean air is more refreshing and revitalizing than that in which we live and breathe in our heated and air-conditioned buildings, but outdoor air is only as good as it is unpolluted. So use your judgment. Also, persons suffering allergies may find filtered or conditioned air more beneficial.

Lastly, obtain regular dental care, and eye care if you need glasses or lenses. Trying to operate your body when important parts are not functioning well adds to your overall stress load and can affect other areas of your health.

Quiz

How are you doing on the health front? Rate yourself by answering yes or no on the chart below.

___ I eat nutritious meals most of the time.

___ I maintain a good weight for my height and body shape.

___ I exercise at least three times a week.

___ I generally get the amount of sleep I need.

___ I get outdoors into the fresh air regularly.

___ I get a dental checkup regularly.

___ I get proper eye care.

___ I rarely get tension headaches.

___ I do not get minor illnesses such as colds and the flu often.

9

Have a Positive Health Attitude

"Look to your health; and if you have it, praise God, and value it next to a good conscience; for health is the second blessing that we mortals are capable of; a blessing that money cannot buy."
——Izaak Walton, *The Compleat Angler*

Good physical health care is more than following a set of habits. A positive health attitude eliminates unnecessary stress when you are ill and assists the healing process. It also prevents health problems from arising.

Be positive about the state of your health. Don't look for a knock in your motor. "If you mean to keep as well as possible, the less you think about your health the better," Oliver Wendell Holmes, dean of Harvard Medical School, said 150 years ago. Everybody has occasional off-days. If one comes your way, assume you are healthy unless you have recognizable symptoms.

If you *are* sick or injured, accommodate your body's needs promptly. Eat appropriately (clear soups, soft foods, or nothing if your digestive tract is disturbed), drink lots of fluids throughout the day, and rest in bed if you are tired. If the medical problem appears serious or you are worrying excessively about your condition, see your doctor. If you just don't feel well, take a watchful stance. Don't push yourself too hard until you know what you are dealing with. "Pamper yourself," a wise doctor once told me. This is not egotistical or selfish; it is just taking good care of your body when your personal needs are high.

Don't run to the doctor for every little ache or pain. Minor medical problems are part of life. Physician/columnist W. Gifford-Jones says, "It's time we all added a bit of grit to our lives." Colds and flu come and go. There isn't much a doctor can do for them. Accept this truth serenely, and seek medical help only if you have a preexisting health condition or if the trouble turns serious and you are threatened with complications.

One of my children began running a low-grade temperature one day. The second day she was ailing, a physician-friend happened to be visiting us. He looked her over and gave her a shot. I believe it just delayed the onset of the medical problem. She went into a physical stall and two weeks later came down with the German measles, which was going around at the time. I often waited a few days before securing medical help for my children. On occasion they would run a slight fever for a few days, only to have it leave later, though unattended. Our bodies heal themselves. God designed them that way. Many times they don't need medicine, only rest and loving care.

Along this line, avoid drugstore remedies for common self-limiting maladies. Dr. Gifford-Jones says, "I've always maintained it's wiser to order chicken soup to treat a cold and that the art of medicine is often to reassure the patient until nature cures the disease." He cautions against overconsuming laxatives: "Thousands of people have crippled their bowels because of laxatives they've consumed and don't need." If constipation occurs frequently, change your dietary habits to include higher bulk foods. If that doesn't help, then see your doctor to find out why.

You can come to know your own body and recognize its trouble signals. Often this is more effective than seeking medical help. A woman had heartburn that no over-the-counter product could help. Her doctor prescribed a stronger medicine, but it too was ineffective. Then she went on vacation and the heartburn left. When she returned home and got back into her usual routine, the problem resumed. The only difference she could see was that while on vacation she had not been drinking her usual cola drinks. She stopped consuming them, and the problem was solved.

Don't take drugs unless you have to, and don't take any more than you have to. Society has been overusing antibiotics, reducing their effectiveness for illnesses where the need is greater. "We've been careless," says Robert Daum, a University of Chicago pediatrician. "Every childhood fever does not require antibiotics." Americans overconsume all kinds of medicines—both prescribed and over-the-counter, experts tell us. Drugs are powerful substances. In and of themselves, they can cause physical disorders. Dean Oliver Wendell Holmes also commented on this problem: "If you tossed all the pills into the Pacific Ocean, so much the better for man, so much the worse for the fish."

On the other hand, if you need medicine to correct a medical problem, to ease severe discomfort, or to function well, take it. Follow the instructions carefully and for as long as the doctor has ordered. Modern medicines can do miracles if taken properly. They are gifts from a loving God to enhance the body's ability to heal itself when that extra help is needed.

Deal Positively with Illness and Pain

When experiencing pain, carry on as cheerfully as possible. You can minimize if not eradicate the misery of pain with a positive mental attitude. Ignore low-level pain—the kind that disappears when you get busy. Medicate appropriately when trying to rest or when the pain builds to a point where it interferes with your ability to function. I have done so for years with a chronic back problem.

Two cautions are needed. First, pain is a warning signal.

It alerts you to an underlying problem. Make certain the problem is identified and treated. Secondly, do not allow pain to build to high, unmanageable levels. It is much harder to bring the pain level down and obtain relief when this happens.

When dealing with pain or illness, you may find yourself overly tired. Pain and illness are stressors. Your body needs extra sleep. Get it. Let others things go.

Don't solve stress problems with drugs unless you are under a doctor's care and he or she orders it. Instead remove the cause or causes of the stress. Otherwise you are just fighting fire with fire.

Do you have emotionally based medical problems? If so, get counseling for the emotional conflict and medicate only as needed until the conflict is resolved. However, if you need antidepressants in order to deal with overwhelming grief, severe depression, or a diagnosed disorder, take them. If you have a serious physical ailment accompanying an emotional conflict, consult a psychiatrist to serve both conditions. They will aggravate each other, pyramiding your health problem and the stress that accompanies it.

Live Right

Prevention is the best medicine, of course, and it is also the best means of minimizing stress in your life. Follow good health and safety habits. Spot serious trouble early by getting regular physical exams and recommended tests. Make sure your shots are up to date. And, to keep your body functioning well, drink lots of water daily. If you don't like it plain, jazz up your glassful with a slice of lemon, lime, or orange. I drink pink lemonade in the summer and herbal teas in cooler weather.

Live right. Avoid overindulging. "If you would live in health, be old early," a Spanish proverb states. Watch your caffeine intake. Don't smoke, and if you drink, drink moderately—not at all if you are pregnant. Stay away from recreational drugs.

Be cautious. Recklessness is glamorous in the movies, but there is a high price to pay. Do *you* want to be the one who pays it? Use seat belts. If you are buying a car, consider purchasing one with airbags, but watch for updated findings about potential cautions. The U. S. Public Health Service advises their use, but they can also cause serious injury if set off accidentally.

Finally, there are two other areas of concern to address. If you need to protect yourself in potentially dangerous situations, pepper sprays or whistles have been found to be safer than guns. And, if you or your husband have a sexually transmitted disease, treat it and use protection, if necessary, to avoid spreading it from one partner to the other.

Avoid Health and Safety Overconcern

"We live in a world of real dangers and imagined fears," says noted columnist Robert J. Samuelson. "We are hounded by . . . 'psycho-facts': beliefs that, though not supported by hard evidence, are taken as real." They are repeated so often, they come to be accepted as true, he says. "We feel assaulted by rising crime, increasing health hazards, falling living standards and a worsening environment. . . . The underlying conditions aren't true, but we feel they are."

Journalists, politicians, policy advocates and promoters of various causes and lifestyles are all heavily implicated in this explosion of misinformation, Samuelson says. "Rarely do any of us deliberately lie. However, we do peddle incomplete or selective information." Such misinformation misleads, inspires exaggeration, and uses improper sources as references, he says. It has often become the basis of misguided public policy.

Journalist Mike Woods of the *Toledo Blade* agrees: "People have a surprisingly distorted sense of the seriousness of various health and environmental risks," he says, claiming that "popular magazines and television programming contribute heavily to these skewed perceptions."

"Are We Scaring Ourselves to Death?" ABC correspondent John Stossel asked on a network special. What do *you* think?

The old adage, *Don't believe everything you read and hear*, has never been so true as today. In environmental and health matters particularly, much of the explosion of scientific data causing great concern is arbitrary. Often the experts don't agree, as in the cholesterol debate. Sometimes new findings overrule the old. For example, asbestos was eventually found to be more dangerous when removed from buildings than when left intact.

Enamored of remarkable twentieth-century achievements and wanting a risk-free world, we are today placing too much confidence in modern scientific methods and testing. Scientific scholarship is valuable if it is authentic and if the testing is carefully carried out. Modern science has without a doubt greatly improved our health and health care and lengthened our life spans. But studies and tests are not absolutes; they have to be weighed in light of their limitations. That does not always happen. Egos often get in the way of good practice in a science-worshiping world.

What we consumers want and need are reliable guidelines for safe and healthful living. How do we find them? We are dismayed when we are told to eat oat bran one year, but learn the next year that it is not the magic cholesterol-fighting miracle portrayed earlier. We lose confidence in the scientific community when one agency tells us herbal supplements are good for us and another says they are not. How can we discern true hazards from overconcern?

First, we need to see science as the inexact discipline it is. By its very nature, testing has self-imposed perimeters. When one group of individuals is studied for cancer caused by smoking, and another nonsmoking control group is set up, that does not necessarily mean that the study results can be applied universally or even that the results are totally valid. There are many variables that could influence the outcome— age, personal habits, genetic makeup, and environmental factors, for instance. It would be nearly impossible to factor all possible variables into every study. Even if scientists could do so, there would still be unknown variables.

Second, recognize the "psycho-facts" problem identified above by Robert Samuelson. Learn to differentiate threats brought by special interest groups or promoted by overeager politicians or journalists from concerns that are legitimate. Look for widespread agreement across several disciplines.

Third, differentiate society's knee-jerk reactions to new developments or crisis situations from widely tested study results and general trends. Much misinformation takes root in the general public because of public overreaction, the desire for a risk-free world, or our present-day inordinate and unrealistic fear of dying. Follow those findings known to be valid. For example, we know without a doubt that car seats save babies' lives. We know reliably that the lead found in old paint is poisonous and should not be used on substances small children might chew.

Fourth, focus on the major risks, such as the dangers from cigarettes and the misuse of alcohol. Don't get caught up by "paper tigers" such as trace chemicals in food and water and rare side effects in prescription drugs. Such low-risk hazards, even if valid, are generally of negligible consequence.

Lastly, give controversial study results the test of time and experience. Ignore the skirmish. Look for the finish. The modern world is in too much of a hurry about everything, including knowledge. Decades ago people used paper covers on public toilet seats to avoid picking up venereal diseases. Later understanding of the way venereal diseases are transmitted proved this practice to be nonessential. When the nuclear cold war got underway, a number of people built and equipped bomb shelters in their basements. This costly, time-consuming effort proved in time to be unnecessary.

However, if you cannot block out of your mind your anxieties on certain issues, follow current thinking in the areas that distress you. Strict accuracy is less important than peace of mind and relief from stress.

10

Cherish the Person You Are

Good health requires more than proper physical care. More than half of all visits to doctors' offices are for psychosomatic disorders. Anxieties, fears, guilt, and phobias can all make us physically ill. Our health and sense of wellness depend a lot on our emotional and spiritual well-being.

The stomach trouble you had the other day might have been caused by a conscience troubled by your perceived neglect of your elderly mother. Peter and I suffered bouts of distress regularly during the eighteen months we housed runaway teenagers for our county. These feelings of distress disappeared as soon as we gave up the job.

Because pressures on women are so heavy today, your need for healthy self-understanding and self-care is magnified. Well-known interior designer and author Alexandra Stoddard says that when you tap into your inner self, you have less need for recognition and assistance from the outside world.

To strengthen yourself emotionally, value and nurture your inner person. Start by accepting yourself. Believe it is okay to be you. It is part of God's plan for your life.

Be yourself. Don't try to be something or someone you are not. Look for *your* strengths, and develop your life around them. Don't try to live up to an ideal that is not realistic or appropriate for you.

Who is your mentor? What characteristics do you admire

about this person? Mine was my mother-in-law. I have never met anyone who accepted other people at face value as well as Jeanne did. In her youth she eloped with Peter's father—an experience she later came to regret. She had hurt her beloved parents deeply. She felt she never again had the right to criticize anyone. As a result, when I was in her presence, I felt like a queen. Nothing I could say or do was unacceptable to her. After her death I learned that all three of her daughters-in-law felt this way. Every one of us believed we were her favorites in the family.

Don't expect to become like your mentor. You are a different person. You bring a differing variety of talents and experiences to life. You can learn from others, but you cannot be them. You can only try to develop the admirable traits of your mentor, to become a better you. I have worked hard to become more nonjudgmental since I came to treasure it so in Jeanne. I have made progress, but only to a point.

Value your uniqueness. This would be a sad and dull world if we did not have distinctive personalities and discernible differences. Just think about that for a moment. Nobody would need anybody! Wouldn't that be disheartening? I have come to treasure my gift of a critical mind. It is a strength that is vital to good writing. Appreciate and build on *your* strengths.

Accept your weaknesses. Modify and work around them. And be advised: our weaknesses are weaknesses only if and when we use them wrongly. My perfectionism once caused me severe stress problems, but it is a welcome asset in my writing.

Value your worth, but not in the way society does. In the public mind, self-worth comes from looks, money (and the things it buys), or accomplishment. Self-esteem that comes from accomplishment feels good for a while, but it does not last. Worth that is founded on one's talents is tenuous; skills can readily be lost in an accident. Handsome facial features can also be lost. And financial reverses can happen to anyone, anytime.

The only sure and lasting esteem comes from valuing who

and what we are in the eyes of God. Humans are the crown of God's creation, superior creatures made by a loving God. God created each of us unique, possessed with assorted gifts—and sometimes given problems—whereby to serve him and humanity. Jesus' disciples once asked who was at fault when a man was born blind, the man or his parents. Jesus answered, "Neither.... he was born blind so that God's works might be revealed in him" (John 9:3). True lasting worth lies in being God's children, redeemed by Christ so we could follow the destiny God has in mind for us.

For Good Emotional Health . . .

Developing emotional control is essential to low stress living. Poise and comfort come hard when our feelings get the better of us. So learn to control your feelings. Don't let them control you.

To acquire control, get in touch with your feelings, honor them, and deal with them. This is easier for some than for others. Some of us have to dig deep to find the source of our distress when we are disturbed. Very often the problem is not where we think it is. Dad comes home from work and yells at the children over a trifle, when his real problem is that he lost a big sale that day. (Dad's problem is not annoyance over noisy children, but disappointment.) I get mad at my husband because he didn't water the new shrubs. The truth is, I am the one who bought them and didn't take care of them and now they are dying. My problem is not with my husband, but myself.

People get in touch with their feelings in different ways. Some talk out their troubles with a friend. Others scrub floors or dig in the garden. Still others jog or retreat to nature. Some people meditate. I journal, putting down whatever pops into my head until my hiding rogues emerge on paper. Find what works for you. A note: wherever your feelings are strongest, that is where your deepest distress lies.

Honor your feelings. Honoring means acknowledging that it is okay to have them. Everyone does, including God, who was often filled with righteous indignation over the sins of his people. Negative feelings are difficult. Anger, sadness, fear, and guilt are unpleasant, embarrassing, and sometimes downright painful. But if we bury them instead of honoring and dealing with them, they come back to haunt us.

The hardest feelings to honor are those we are ashamed to admit to, especially for sincere Christians. Do you hate your mother at times because she is a controller and won't let you make decisions for yourself? Are you angry with your child because he has been getting you up during the night lately without good reason? These feelings are valid and temporary. They are based on behaviors, not persons. You have a right to be upset when someone else's actions impact negatively on your life. Being angry does not mean that you have done something wrong or have stopped loving that person. God certainly hasn't, or we would all be sunk.

To deal with your feelings, decide what to do about them. Contrary to what was thought years ago, we do not have to punch somebody or verbally blast off. What's needed is to mentally acknowledge our feelings and decide how to handle them.

It is best and least stressful to let minor annoyances roll off our backs like water over a waterfall. Some things are not worth troubling over. We all need to overlook the little quirks of those we live with, lest we be forever complaining or nagging. With feelings too strong to dismiss, talk things over with the offending person. Since interpersonal conflicts are one of our greatest sources of distress, in a later chapter I will cover in depth how to handle them.

Strong positive feelings can also stress us. Family members go into a high gear when there is a family wedding—especially a big one. Significant accomplishments also stress. The day my first book contract arrived, I walked around the house in a daze for hours.

You can learn how to handle strong positive stresses gracefully. The stress of weddings or large parties is usually caused by worry that something will go wrong, so plan ahead carefully. However, since you can't prevent everything that could possibly go wrong, decide at the same time to enjoy yourself, come what may. I now mentally shift gears, drop my schedule, call my dearest friends, and dine out with my family on days when exciting news comes. What is an especially delightful treat for you? This is the time to indulge it.

Finally, for good emotional health, accept responsibility for yourself. Many of our conflicts are caused not by what others do to us, but by what we do to ourselves. It is my fault if I get upset with my teenager because she has frequent arguments with me. She is just learning to express her independence. She needs to, at this point in her life. Expecting her to agree with me is unreasonable.

Don lost big money when his business went bankrupt. He blamed his partner, who walked out and left him fully responsible for a $55,000 tax liability. Don was distraught until a psychiatrist showed him that a large share of the fault lay with him, for leaving himself legally vulnerable for the full debt.

Work on your bad habits. Are you a chronic late-arriver? Launch a plan that will help you get places on time. Are you angry that you watched a good late show on television last night and didn't get enough sleep to assure you a good day? Set a firm bedtime and commit to it, regardless of the programming. It is easier to live with and accept yourself if you are working on your weaknesses. Then you can say to yourself when you slip up now and then, "At least I'm trying."

If you are having great difficulty identifying or working through negative feelings or if you cannot function well due to emotional stresses, obtain counseling help. Many people avoid it, thinking that using counseling services means you are weak or don't trust God enough. Not so. Our family went for counseling when a teenage daughter went out of control, when our adopted child was having emotional problems, and when a member of our family was suffering from an addiction. Counseling is a twentieth-century gift from God given to lighten some of the greatest distresses in living. Enrich your life. Use it.

Make certain your counselor is helpful to you. Our family once consulted a minister who told us what my husband and

I wanted to hear, but our troubled relationship with our teenage daughter only worsened. Good therapy is often painful. The bottom line is, are you getting the results you want?

Nourish Your Soul Regularly

For wellness and good stress control, our souls need to be fed regularly, just as our bodies do. Physicians increasingly agree that strong spiritual beliefs are crucial to emotional well-being and general good health. A 1994 National Institutes of Health report asked the entire medical community to lift their traditional prohibition against probing the beliefs of their patients, acknowledging that "religious and spiritual meanings are correlated with increased physical and mental health."

Keep in close touch with God by practicing faithfully a life of worship and service. Include in your worship regular visits to the communion table. Weekly worship draws us close to God frequently and exposes us regularly to God's value system. This is vital during these times when wholesome spiritual values differ so markedly from those we push up against constantly in the secular world. If you must drop something from a too busy, hectic schedule, drop something else. Soul food pays for itself.

Methodist Bishop Cushman, in setting forth "Holy Habits for Christians," says giving a fixed portion of your income is another important element in spiritual health. We need to give something back to God and his purposes, not just receive. Cushman recommends tithing and suggests that the giver put this money aside when the paycheck first comes in. All the tithers I have ever met were happy people, regardless of income level. I have found that God rewards generously those who remember him and support his work.

Bible studies and spiritual retreats provide spiritual food in depth. A psalmist said, "(God's) word is a lamp to my feet and a light for my path" (Psalm 119:105). There is no easier, better way to draw close to the Lord.

We also see God in people, according to Mother Teresa, who claimed to see Christ in the lowliest outcasts of Calcutta. If you are not already doing so, give some time to helping the less fortunate. Nothing is as good for us as giving loving care to our fellow human beings. It gets our minds off our problems, our self-centeredness, and our self-indulgence. Loving others and serving their needs not only helps them, but also balances the social scales of our lives.

Service to God's church and humanity can overload us, however. Some of us, feeling overly responsible for "carrying our share of the load," disregard personal needs or skimp on family time. God does not want that. We have to set appropriate limits. A friend of mine, the mother of six children, limited her involvements to one church and one community-related organization at a time.

Even that may be too much for some. I have had to say no a number of times since I began writing; writing requires long uninterrupted hours of concentration, which are as tiring as physical labor. A Christian writer I know declines all organized church work, explaining, "*Writing* is my ministry." Do what you can do, and limit yourself to that. That is all God asks of you. For peace of mind, ask God in prayer to guide your decision.

Take Time for Personal Needs

See to your personal needs, tight as your schedule may be. Time spent on personal care is well invested. It energizes you for the other areas of your life.

Plan enough time to fix your hair in a way that pleases you. If you believe your hair looks nice, it will lift your spirits all day long. Similarly, take time for bathing and for the selection and care of your wardrobe. Even your "grubbies" can make you feel good about yourself if they are attractive. You can minimize the time investment by selecting easy-care clothing and limiting the size of your wardrobe if necessary. Fewer items mean less time spent keeping them up.

Just as your body and soul need to be fed, so does your mind. You are what you think about all day long. Feed your mind healthy food. Read constructive material and think healthy thoughts. Cross out of your life those things—television shows, books, magazines, song lyrics, plays, or whatever—that reflect unwholesome values.

Give yourself some personal time. This also energizes. What interests do you have that are distinctly your own? Reading? Crafts? Sports? Music? Photography? Choose at least one to indulge in. I attend church choir faithfully, not just as a service to God and my church, but because I find it so relaxing. Wednesday night rehearsals are a thirst-quenching oasis in the middle of my week.

Take time for personal friends. Friends are important to emotional health and wholeness. At a women's conference I attended several years ago, the leader played a game with the audience. "Write down the five most important things in your life, in order of importance," she said. My answers were: God, husband, children, friends, writing. "Now take the least important one away," she said.

What a crucible she put us through, to have to make a decision like that! One by one we had to drop off our entries. Taking some time, I agonizingly dropped my children and writing first. Then I hit an amazing snag. I was shocked to realize that I needed my friends more than my husband. If he died, I would still have my friends to support me. But if they were gone, I would have only him—one person—along with God to help me cope with all the problems of life. It was a telling reality. This was merely an experiment in determining true needs, of course. My husband actually is my best friend. But it taught me that personal friendships are vital, and nurturing them is a high priority item. I learned some time ago that we cannot expect any one person to meet all of our needs every time we have needs. It was a lesson on the importance of community.

Set aside time to relax, even if it's only a ten-minute treat. Rest, even in small doses, revitalizes not only your body but your mind and soul. What activities enable you to relax? Reading? Strolling around the block? Visiting your library? Sitting in the back yard and taking in nature? Listening to soft music? Soaking in a bubble bath? Work your choice into your schedule—daily, if possible. Call it "my time."

Quiz

How good are your emotional health habits? Rate yourself from 1 - 5, with 1 being low, and 5 high.

___ I like myself.

___ I control my emotions well most of the time.

___ I don't hang on to resentments, anger, or guilt.

___ I take adequate time for my personal care needs.

___ I feed my mind good food.

___ I feed my soul faithfully.

___ I take time to serve the needs of the less fortunate.

___ I find time for my interests.

___ I make time for my friends.

___ I relax easily.

___ I enjoy my life.

11

Listen to the Voices within You

A number of years ago I began to suffer repeated bouts of stomach trouble. Anxieties over family financial pressures, anemia, and a lengthy spate of illnesses in our three-year-old daughter were pressing in on me like a vise. One night it all came down. In a matter of hours my mind was besieged and overwhelmed by a raging, unstoppable flood of irrational fears: "You are going to die." "Your family is going bankrupt." "Susie is going to die."

"These hellish thoughts make no sense," I kept telling myself. I had just had a physical and checked out free of serious problems. My husband, a life insurance agent, had had a temporary shortfall in sales, pinching a tight just-getting-started budget, but he was already back on track. Susie had developed an intense heart murmur as a result of her barrage of illnesses, but it was temporary and her tests showed she had sustained no heart damage. Yet my rationalizing did no good. The threats just kept coming.

The siege lasted three days and four nights. "Why *now*?" I asked my pastor, when they began to ease. "Why *now*, when things are finally coming together for us again." "Delayed stress," he told me. It is when we begin to let go after a trauma that it starts taking its emotional toll on us. In my case, that toll was clinical depression, or burnout.

Sporadic bouts of depression returned for several months. I soon realized that my depression was caused by physical and emotional exhaustion—the result of poor stress management.

Stress management is essential to good general health and well-being. If allowed to pyramid, stress can devastate us. My sudden descent into depression shattered my self-confidence. My hope was destroyed (a characteristic of severe depression, even when the hopeless feelings are unwarranted by circumstances). My body chemistry altered, and for nearly a year I was unable to function at my normal level.

It was a terrifying condition. During this time I began to understand why people commit suicide: It is welcome relief from that kind of pain. Sometimes, I discovered, it is harder to go on living than it is to face death.

As I recovered, I began to look at factors that had contributed to my illness. I didn't take care of myself, even when the warning signals came. I had seen the stresses building for months. I recognized that I was getting more and more exhausted, but I told myself I could handle it. A friend of mine had troubles greater than mine, and she was coping well. If she could cope, so could I!

I didn't listen to my inner self, and my refusal to respond to my limitations led to disaster. Perhaps that is why I felt called to write this book. I would like to save others this debilitating kind of torment.

Causes of Stress Illness

The stresses that undo us are not caused by our jobs or families or schedules. We do these things to ourselves. Months before my breakdown, I started to notice that I had to sit down while teaching nursery school. As the months went on, the sit-down time increased. Obviously I was getting more and more fatigued.

At that point I could have dropped other responsibilities— my role as Girl Scout troop leader, for instance. I told myself I had to keep going because "no one else will do it." I could have quit teaching; but I told myself we needed the money.

We had already gone into debt twice starting a new business, and I didn't want to do it again. But we would have managed. If we couldn't, that would just indicate that the Lord wanted something else for us. As it was, I had to stop teaching anyway when the depression hit.

Inflexibility adds to stress. My illness was aggravated by a rigid perfectionist personality. I have since been learning to modify it, in self-defense. I do so gladly. Dr. Menninger of the famed Menninger Clinic has said that breakdowns are good for us because the experience motivates us to become more flexible. The reed that bends is less apt to break under pressure. And, I must add, it enables us to accept and enjoy life more.

Another contributor to my stress illness was my tendency to think *I* had to do it all. How ridiculous! No one can do everything. We all need to lean on other people at times for assistance. Furthermore, letting others help or take over gives them a rewarding opportunity to serve someone else's needs.

I tended to worry a lot. It is fruitless to become anxious about things that may never happen. Jesus told us to take a lesson from the lilies of the fields and the birds. Carefree, they let God nourish and care for them.

I was always planning ahead. We all need to do that, of course, to some extent. Life is more enjoyable when we have something special to look forward to, whether it be a vacation trip or redecorating the bedroom. However, I was forever living in the future, not quite content with the present. I always wanted a little more than we had. A bigger house. Better cars. More money to buy more things. I lacked appreciation for my present blessings. This kind of thinking is unhealthy. The product of such a mindset is chronic discontent. Not a nice place to be.

Another contributor to my stress illness was my lack of attention to a physical ailment—anemia. Since this was something I fought chronically due to heavy menstrual periods, I didn't let the special needs it brought concern me. This too is unhealthy. Even minor ailments and illnesses—colds, sore muscles, headaches—take a stressful toll on us. If we don't pay attention, our neglect of ourselves can come back to haunt us.

The Pressures on Women Today

The pressures on women today are as great if not greater than when I fell ill. Career burnout occurs in the workplace. Women everywhere are expressing dissatisfaction with the overall workload they feel they must handle.

Cultural expectations are part of the problem. Society still presumes that modern women can manage well an active life filled with work, family, care of the home, and personal time. This is just not realistic. A 1995 *Newsweek* article stated, "Experts say the toughest occupation [stress-wise] may still be that of working mom. Many women who are bringing home the bacon are still expected to fry and serve it, too." Harriet Lerner of the Menninger Clinic says, "There really are relatively few couples where child care and domestic work are truly shared." In the divorced and other single parent families so prevalent today, there *is* no other adult to share the workload and the day-to-day responsibility. Until cultural expectations change, women who would reduce the stress in their lives must fight this Superwoman mentality—in themselves and in society, as well as in their families.

To deal with stress well, we need to understand its nature. A certain amount of stress is normal and is present with us all the time. We need and benefit from a little added stress (we call it "getting psyched up") in order to concentrate and do well when undertaking mental and physical efforts—taking a test, giving a speech, or performing in a stage play, for instance. It is only when we allow our lives to become too tense or overloaded that it becomes a problem for us. The result can range from mild (I am too nervous to score well on this test) to severe (burnout).

It can happen to any of us. Harvard University President Neil Rudenstine hit the burnout wall. The detail-oriented Rhodes scholar dozed through his morning schedule one day, two years after taking on his prestigious position. Realizing that he was juggling too many balls, he reduced his schedule for several weeks. Exhausted again a year later from a still too-frantic schedule, he overslept one morning. Now Rudenstine knew that he was experiencing serious burnout. During a three-month sabbatical, he was able to sort things out and realize he had to back off and delegate more responsibility.

A casual attitude toward occasional minor stress overload will help you deal with it. Expect that, life being what it is, it is going to happen now and then. All of us run frantic once in a while.

When an occasional overload creeps up on you, recognize that it is temporary. Knowing that makes it easier to put up with a transient situation. Also, have those around you (coworkers or family) help you find ways to deal with the problems that crop up as a result. Sharing a problem makes it easier to handle, and others' input may give you solutions you had not thought of.

Ask yourself whether your stress is coming from your *reaction* to the situation you are in, or from the situation itself. You can change your reaction and still get relief, even if you cannot change the situation.

When life's high-stress times come, stop in your tracks and back off from the situation for several minutes, or an hour, or a day. If you are in the midst of severe trauma, take a trip for a week or two or take a leave of absence from your job. It takes time and distance from life's stressful demands to rebuild emotional energies.

Get away from the scene. During my depression on my bad days my husband took me to the store—any store—just to get me out of the house. It took me out of myself and back into life.

Talk out your feelings, as you get to where you can handle them. Our son left home unexpectedly before he had completed high school. Peter and I, deeply discouraged, went camping at a nearby state park. Walking through the woods and hiking the sunlit trails, we were able to share and begin to assuage our disappointment.

Choose a quiet, peaceful place. As we talked, Peter and I reveled in the glory of God's creation. Meeting God in his untouched natural world has a tremendous healing effect on me, I have found.

When living under high-stress conditions, it is particularly important to balance your life. Drop nonessentials, tend to vital business, exercise, spend some quality time with your family, get needed rest, pray at every turn, and laugh at yourself and at life's unreasonable demands. This will help you keep your sanity.

Stress Management

To manage stress well, know yourself and how you cope. Do you listen to the voices within you? Are you alert to your body signals? Can you identify your flash point—what happens when things are starting to get to you? Can you point out your hidden reefs (situations where you unexpectedly erupt into rage)? I overreact to manipulation, probably because I am gullible and slow to pick up on it when it occurs.

How well do you recognize your coping strategies? Do you know how to handle stress triggers gracefully when they surface? "I need to talk about this" works in some situations. Taking a coffee break to get away from the problem may help. Getting physical is helpful with severe jolts. Scrubbing floors, weeding the garden, tackling a paint job, or punching a pillow are harmless ways to siphon off simmering or exploding energies.

What techniques work best for you and under what circumstances? Lesser problems will call for different strategies than serious problems. Give this area some thought. If you are conscious of your coping strategies, you can turn to them more quickly when the need for them arises.

Quiz

How well are you doing on the stress meter? Answer M for most of the time, S for sometimes, or N for not often or never.

____ I am allowing my career aspirations and longing for success to stress my life.

____ I am letting my desire to maintain a high standard of living squeeze my personal life and time.

___ I worry about everything—even things that might not happen.

___ I feel I have to keep going, even when I get upset or don't feel up to par.

___ I find it difficult to change my plans.

___ I believe I *must* get the house cleaned every week.

___ I prefer to do everything myself rather than ask for help.

___ I think it is important to "keep my chin up," even if that means I am carrying a too-heavy burden.

___ I live for tomorrow, when things will get better.

Fill out the following information about your coping skills.

My body _____

_____ when I am stressed.

When things are getting to me, my mind _____

_____

I can't talk about _____

_____

_____.

I get angry if people bring up_____

_____.

I deal with minor frustrations by (list several) _____

_____

_____.

When bad things happen, I cope by _____

_____

_____

_____.

Stress-relieving Emotional Health Habits

During my first several months of recovery, I realized I had to change my way of thinking to avoid trouble again. My mental roadmap had led me into deep, treacherous waters. Here is the new one I laid down. It is an excellent guide for good emotional health. None of these were on my list before my depression. All of them were, shortly thereafter.

1. *Live for today.* You cannot do anything about the past. It is history. You cannot forecast the future. Even if you plan for tomorrow, circumstances beyond your sight or control may change your plans. The only place you can surely make a difference is today.

2. *Count your blessings.* When my depression hit, money was tight. We were just getting started in a difficult profession. The house needed a coat of paint. The children needed winter boots. We were late in getting a few bills paid. I felt God was letting us down. "People who are putting their trust in God should not be getting behind on utility bills," I told myself.

As I recovered, I began to see how ungrateful I was. We had never missed a house payment. We had good, nourishing food on the table three times a day. We were keeping ahead of car payments on a late model car and the high gasoline bills that were essential in my husband's business. We had much love in our household, happy relationships, and many material blessings. My ingratitude was caused by my rigid goals, not God's faithlessness.

3. *Expect change.* If work runs the wheels of living, change is the windmill that provides the energy.

Change is inevitable. Thank God it is. We hate to see good times pass, but the chance is always there that more good times will come. When change comes during bad times, it brings hope. "This too shall pass," a comforting friend told me in the midst of my depression.

4. *Listen to the voices within you.* To avert or minimize stress illness, recognize and respond promptly to the over-stresses in your life. When your inner voice tells you to lighten the load or change procedures, follow through.

5. *Respect your limitations.* Don't try to change what you cannot change.

You can change some circumstances; others you cannot. You can change jobs if your boss makes your working conditions intolerable, but you cannot change the situation itself unless higher-ups are willing to listen to your complaints. You can buy another car if yours breaks down, but you can't make your car keep running if it's too old and worn out. You can move if the new neighbors make noise half the night, or ask them for some consideration; but you can't make them quiet down if they don't want to. Even if you call the police, they may start up again after the patrol car leaves the scene. You can ask the police or courts to take action, but is it worth it? Would that accomplish what you want?

You cannot change other people, but you can change yourself. If your spouse or the person you are dating is not romantic, you can't make him romantic, but you can decide that romance is not as important as faithfulness. You cannot make your rebellious teenager compliant, but you can listen carefully and try to respond to this child's urgent needs and concerns. As the serenity prayer so wisely says, "God, give me the serenity to accept the things I cannot change, the courage to change the things I can, and the wisdom to know the difference."

6. *Seek support from others.* You cannot do everything alone. You cannot face every problem that comes along without moral support. God does not expect you to. As recorded in the New Testament, God sent companions with Paul on all of his missionary journeys.

Two theme songs weave steadily in and out of the New Testament apostolic letters: "Encourage one another in the faith" and "Bear one another's burdens." We need one another. We also need to help one another. What a beautiful social plan! Not only does support from others make our workloads lighter and ease our anxieties, but it is also more fun to be with people than to be alone.

7. *Lean on God.* No one person can be there for us every time we need to unburden our hearts. Your pastor might be on vacation. (Doesn't it always happen that way?) Your dearest friend may not be home when a troubling situation crops up. But God is always there to lean on.

When my depression hit, I couldn't relate to anyone. "No one can understand what I am going through," I said to myself over and over again. I knew no one who had. But I could lean on God. The one sure thread I could cling to was the knowledge that God loved me and would help me. God was my lifeline.

Make God *your* lifeline.

12

Adopt Easy-living Attitudes and Perspectives

"Much of life is in the attitude," says Dr. W. Gifford-Jones in his medical advice column.

As the 1864 presidential election approached, President Lincoln was asked, "What will you do if Ulysses S. Grant's capture of Richmond is followed by his nomination and acceptance of the candidacy?"

"Well," Lincoln responded, "I feel very much like the man who said he didn't want to die particularly, but if he had to die, that was precisely the disease he would like to die of."

It's all in the attitude.

We humans are complex beings. We have distinctive personalities. Our lives are shaped by varying experiences, including the painful ones. But other factors come into play when we look at how and when stress affects us. Two other foundation stones of stress management are the attitudes and perspectives we bring to life, to ourselves, and to the world around us.

Psychologists tell us that we react according to preset tapes in our heads. These tapes—our thinking and behavior patterns—are acquired during our growing-up years. How many times have you said to someone, "You act just like your father (or mother)"?

Since these tapes are learned, we can relearn those that don't do a good job for us. *Attitudes* are mindsets. They drive our *thoughts*. If I want to have a positive, upbeat attitude toward life, I will think of my mistakes as growing experiences. Thoughts give birth to *emotions*. If I believe mistakes make people failures, I will feel diminished by mine. Our thoughts and emotions, working together continuously, become the habits that steer our actions and behaviors.

It stands to reason, then, that if unwanted stress is diminishing or controlling your life, the best way to generate better results is to start at the headwaters—your attitudes about your wants, needs, and obligations. Mental attitudes can be reversed or modified to prevent or reduce stress. Certain thinking habits can keep you from walking unnecessarily into many stressful situations.

Here are some attitudes and thinking habits that ease stress in our general approach to living.

To Prevent Stress . . .

Squash thoughts of self-pity. The worst habit a person can get into is to dwell on problems endlessly. Life isn't fair. It doesn't have to be. You can be happy doing your best with the lot you are given. You won't be happy feeling you have been treated unfairly, and you will only make others around you miserable. No one likes being around complainers. No one gains from it.

Decide not to indulge in self-pity, even if you have just cause. The antidote to feeling sorry for yourself is to keep busy. It makes your trouble easier to bear because it takes your mind off your plight. My advice from my doctor when I was diagnosed with depression was, "Get back to work as soon as you can."

Stifle unwarranted fears. Stop worrying about things you cannot control or do anything about. You cannot change the fact that your family has a history of early deaths due to heart disease. You cannot change a world in turmoil. What you *can* do is take good care of yourself and leave the rest, including the world's troubles, in God's hands. "Cast all your anxiety on him, because he cares for you" (1 Peter 5:7).

Don't get trapped by unearned guilt. You are not responsible for pleasing other people, for meeting their goals, or for doing everything they ask of you. You are accountable only to God and to the responsibilities God gives you. Anything else is a matter of choice—yours.

Dispense with unwanted obligations. Get in the habit of saying no. If you can't say no on the spot, ask to think about it. This gives you time to build up the courage to say no later.

Ignore undeserved criticism. When others find fault with you, search your mind and heart. If the criticism is deserved, thank the person for helping you. Valid criticism is helpful; it shows us where we can improve. However, if you are satisfied that you carried through properly, put the matter out of mind. Other persons could have a problem with you— jealousy, perhaps. That's their problem. Don't make it your problem.

Are you victimized by prejudice or discrimination? Follow the same self-evaluation process. If your complaint is justified, you may decide to seek justice—but count the cost. If the price is too high stress-wise, fight your battle in less stressful ways or chalk it up to "This is the world I live in today and I'll have to be satisfied with a less-than-perfect world." None of us—even Christian believers—escapes the fallout of sin, or our own contribution to it.

Put out of your life stressful persons, meetings, and situations, where possible. If a neighbor, coworker, or member of your family seems antagonistic toward you for no apparent reason, be pleasant but distant. You will never get along with everyone, and it is not always necessary to try to work things out. Tell yourself, "Life is too short for this," and let it go. If the Bible study you attend is mostly a gossip session, find another group. With persons you cannot walk away from, follow the suggestions in chapter 15 on conflict resolution.

Refuse to accept unwanted intrusions into your life such as salespersons at the door and telephone solicitors. You do not owe such a caller the courtesy of your time. You have the right to refuse *any* unsolicited entries into your life—even phone calls from friends and acquaintances who drop in at inappropriate times. In certain situations (sickness, family conferences) it may be beneficial and important to ask them to call or visit later.

Use telephone answering machines to control intrusive telephone calls. To prevent junk mail, turn in your name to Mail Preference Service, Direct Marketing Association, P.O. Box 3861, New York, NY 10163-3861 and request that your name not be sold to list companies. This should reduce your mail by 75 percent. Also, ask the catalog companies you use not to sell your name.

Use the answering machine for obscene phone callers; they don't get satisfaction if no one answers. If this doesn't suffice, change to an unlisted number.

Cut short hangers-on—those people who can't end a phone conversation or leave your home at the end of a party. You won't hurt any feelings if you say something like, "I'm sorry, I really have to call it a day."

To Minimize Stress when Difficulties Arise . . .

Be alert to your red flag days. If you are struggling with PMS or if you've simply had a bad day at work, be extra careful what you say and do and pamper yourself a bit. Ask your family to give you extra consideration. Have your teenagers turn down the volume on their boom boxes if the noise bothers you. Let them cook supper for a change.

Don't give second wind to mistakes and failures. When you slip up, decide how you can do better, and then forget about it.

When you get in a bind, take your time. Back off, rethink, and redo.

Always have a Plan B handy. My back was aching the day I hosted a writer's club meeting. Instead of baking my favorite pie, I bought donut holes and, for added "treat appeal," served them with ice cream floats. The unusual menu went over great.

Dig into a load of difficulties one at a time. Break the stress mountain down into manageable hills. Begin with the most pressing or immediate problem. When that one is resolved, go after the next. Nearly any tower of difficulties can be managed if we go at it this way.

Tackle monstrous challenges one day at a time. Or one hour at a time, if you are facing major surgery or waiting out a critical illness in a family member. This works! Ask any person recovering from an addiction.

Screen and disregard cultural messages that violate your beliefs and values. We cannot prevent modern society from going its excessive route in the name of freedom. While some may choose to fight it, those wanting an easier-stress route can rest in the knowledge that self-indulgence—whether it be in sex, drugs, or greed—eventually turns in on and kills itself. Decide not to be its victim by avoiding exposure to those messages.

Look at ups and downs as challenges to be met. Life is a struggle. Pure idealists are doomed to live with constant disappointment. But we needn't be pessimists either. It's a matter of attitude and balance.

Express your good feelings as they occur. This will brighten your disposition and boost your own spirits as well as those of others. We all can use more sunshine in our lives.

Lighten Your Perspectives on Life

Another powerful force in managing stress is found in our perspectives, or mental views about life. How you see yourself, others, life, and the world around you can lift you up or pull you down. Your mental views can inspire, discourage, motivate, or depress you. For low-stress living, build on perspectives that are positive for "lift value," realistic for solid grounding, comforting for ease, and satisfying for enjoyment of living.

How do these perspectives match up with yours?

Think positive thoughts.

Do you look at the world through rose-colored glasses? Is your cup of life half-empty or half-full? "Half-fullers" look forward to life. They exude optimism, hope, and trust in the future. Life is lighter, fuller, and richer for them. When half-fullers fail, they learn from their failures. When they suffer hurt, they grow from their hurts. They enjoy life more. So will you, if you choose to be one of them.

View life with optimistic realism.

Archbishop Fulton Sheen once said, "Nothing is more destined to create deep-seated anxieties in people than the false assumption that life should be free from anxieties." Do you expect ups and downs as a part of life? Are you avoiding the truth that death is a certainty none of us escapes? Can you accept these truths with grace?

Society is no help; it shuns these realities. There is a pill for every ailment, even though with the most common ones—colds and flu—medicine doesn't help much if at all. Society encourages us to fight heart diseases at all cost, even among the frail elderly, though a heart attack or a massive stroke is an easier way to die than the other big cause of death—cancer.

Facing reality would seem to accelerate rather than relieve stress, but oddly, the opposite is true. We enjoy life more when we acknowledge that we go through life only once and must therefore make each day count. We relieve stress when we admit we can handle only so much. We are more relaxed and easier to live with when we admit we are human and fallible. (Incidentally, people like us better, too.)

We Christians can face even the unbearable with grace by leaning on God instead of our limited selves. God promises to be there for us. I have never known a believer to say that the Lord ever let him or her down, if that person was actively seeking his help during a crisis. God may not answer prayers the way we want, but he invariably helps us cope. God is always there for me and often provides far more than I expect or even hope for.

Consider death, suffering, and aging a normal part of life.

Many of our anxieties today arise from our irrational, senseless fear of death. Death is a part of life. For Christians, it is a door opening to eternal life with a God who loves us and a precious reunion with departed loved ones. Most elderly persons welcome death. My husband's grandmother, in good health and of right mind, said one day that she had lived long enough. Now that Grandpa was gone, she too was ready to meet her Maker. The thought shocked me at the time, but now I see how well-adjusted she was. As it happened, she lived for several more years.

Suffering is another of life's unmentionables. With so many medicines available to ease much of life's discomfort, we tend to think people should not have to hurt anymore. That, too, is unrealistic. Though modern medical science has made numerous advances, many health and pain issues remain unsolved. Well-adjusted persons expect occasional discomfort and, if faced with chronic pain problems, learn how to cope.

Aging is inevitable. In eastern societies, age is venerated. Age brings wisdom. Older persons lose their vanities and gain a greater acceptance of life. My Bible study group was once asked if we would like to go back to what we were ten years earlier. None of those persons aged forty and older said yes. Only in a youth-worshiping society such as ours is aging something to be avoided at all cost. If you decide not to fear it, you will enjoy the tradeoff. Older persons lose, but they also gain.

Give yourself, life, and people some slack.

Are you upset with yourself at times? It happens to all of us. Go easy on yourself. Recognize that we all make changes when we want to badly enough. So will you. Until then, don't sweat it. Don't smile if you don't feel like smiling. Contrary to popular opinion, fake smiles are failures. They kid no one. It's okay to be sad on your bad days. Caring people would rather you were honest than pretending to be pleasant.

In every race and nation—and almost every family—you will find some good and some extremely bad behaviors. A number of years ago I helped resettle a family from Laos. The father of the family was dismayed with a brother who had tried to seduce his wife. Yet the man I was dealing with was obviously honorable. We agreed: this kind of family situation is typical of the human race.

Don't let the nature of media material distort your faith in people. The media print and broadcast bad news because, unfortunately, that is what most readers, viewers, and listeners prefer. The truth is, most people are good and kind. More than half of all Americans are church members in a nation where church membership is voluntary. Enormous outpourings of love occur when tragedies strike our country. Listen to people talk about their experiences and their families. Notice how many large corporations respond generously to community needs.

Cut slack also with people who seem to fall short of their responsibilities. People generally do the best they can in their circumstances. I have known personally a number of troubled youths and several adults who were stuck on welfare. They were truly down and out, and our helping systems were not meeting their needs effectively. Though laziness and fraud are always present in the system, most people come around when someone, or society, finds an adequate way to help them.

Give society some slack.

Modern society has gone overboard in its criticism of people and systems. For lower-stress living, avoid judging. History is most accurately seen in the perspective of the times and situations of the people living them. Follow the old Native American adage: Don't judge a man until you have walked in his moccasins for a day.

Cut slack regarding the solving of societal problems by recognizing that our society is aware of and working on its deficiencies. We will never have it all together because one problem solved usually creates another one elsewhere. Society still cares and will keep trying. That is what really matters.

If and when that changes—and that possibility appears to be on the horizon—that is when we truly need to be concerned and to pray even harder for our country. In the last few decades it has become more and more acceptable to be preoccupied with self-interest and to deny any responsibility for the welfare of our local, national, or world community. The Lord has told us differently: "Do not use your freedom as an opportunity for self-indulgence, but through love become slaves to one another" (Galatians 5:13b). We are called as a society to love and take care of one another.

It is hard to give slack to politicians who listen more carefully to their party leaders, campaign supporters, and lobbyists than to their constituents. But no political system is without its deficiencies. Fortunately, living in a democratic country, we can continue to refine our government. In time we may come up with something that will work better. But that too will have its disadvantages. Thus it is good that political change takes place slowly, for we have a better chance of finding effective and lasting solutions.

Keep your world-view in perspective.

From time to time we hear threats of pending global disaster—global warming, loss of the ozone layer, a world-wide AIDS epidemic, and the like. As with the medical and safety psycho-facts mentioned in an earlier chapter, they can rob us of our tranquility.

Keep these threats in perspective. Charles Krauthammer in *Time* magazine identifies them as "periodic enthusiasms that wash over the culture." He considers these risks magnified, terms them "intellectual fads," and advises people not to lose their heads. Some people find it helpful to counteract their anxieties about the state of the globe by becoming proactive rather than reactive with their world-view. Instead of passively accepting the world as it is, they become activists for a favorite cause. That is a positive way to cope. "Look outward," Krauthammer suggests. Seek to serve the needs of those around you instead of becoming self-absorbed in potential disasters that probably never will occur.

Another way to keep these things in perspective is to remember that God is in control of this universe. It will survive as long as God wants it to, even if every hostile nation develops a nuclear bomb.

As a last resort, when your community bends under the

101

weight of heinous crime—as mine did with the kidnapping, sexual assault, and murder of a twelve-year-old girl—pray and keep your eyes on the long view. We don't know why such things happen or how a loving God can allow it. But we can take precautions and pray for protection for ourselves and our loved ones. We can rest assured that society is working hard to secure justice and that God has promised us that evil will not go unpunished. Even though we don't understand, we can remember what St. Paul told us: "In everything God works for good with those who love him" (Romans 8:28, RSV).

Picture yourself as a calm and gentle spirit.

Regardless of your personality, you can train yourself to remain calm and collected in all but the most sudden trying situations. To acquire a gentle spirit, take time to make reasoned decisions; then decide to act on them with tender firmness and compassion. A feisty demeanor or combative manner won't make your life easier or assure you even-handed interaction. In fact it may prolong difficulties with others. Any matters can be managed well and less stressfully by combining grace with love. "The effect of righteousness will be peace, and the result of righteousness, quietness and trust forever" (Isaiah 32:17).

The rest of this book will address practical ways to reduce the stress in your family, home, and leisure life.

13

Make Time for Your Family

"Juggling work and family is a constant challenge," says Sue Simonson, a parochial school teacher and administrator. "Any person, mother, wife, in any career, questions at times whether she is letting her career override her family."

How true. We women today can get so caught up in the demands of jobs and the details of living that we lose sight of what really matters. Focusing on priorities takes time and a distancing we find hard pressed to come by.

To minimize stress and enjoy life more, stay focused. Regarding your family, get in the habit of asking yourself regularly, "How are we as a family handling our present lifestyle? Is it working for us? Where are we headed? Is this what we—and I—want for us?" And lastly, "What is my goal in all of this?"

The ideal is a happy, fulfilled mom, or wife and mom. She can be a working person, an active volunteer, or an at-home mom. She can be one who spends quantity time or quality time with her family, but she has time for what matters. She has no guilt about her present role in life because she has been and is steadily continuing to work it out with God.

She makes family life number one on her involvement list because caring for her family is a God-given responsibility. Though God assigned a work role to Adam and Eve in Paradise, he also created the family as the basic social unit in the created world. Both roles must be held in creative balance in the lives of God's people.

Is this ideal attainable? New Jersey Governor Christine Todd Whitman would say yes. This is how she managed to raise two healthy, happy, well-adjusted children while working and living in the public eye: "I always maintained one guiding principle: the family comes first. That meant not being afraid to postpone a meeting because of an important child-related activity. It meant always carving out a time of the day to do something together. In our case, it was reading to the children every morning at breakfast and at night before bed."

Stress specialist Dr. Steven Klein, speaking to married couples, said he also believes it can be done, though it is not easy. "Having a fulfilling career can provide both members of the couple with higher self-esteem and a greater sense of self worth, not to speak of financial gain," says Dr. Klein. "On the other hand, the demands of the two-career lifestyle, from housework to child care and time pressures, can take a big toll." He goes on to say that the old rules no longer apply. "Dual-earners must create new rules that work for them."

Give Time to Your Marriage

One of the major time/stress problems in today's world is a lack of intimacy and communication between married couples, Dr. Klein says. "[Couples] come to me and tell me they have no time for fun, for sex, for doing the things they like to do." They burn up all their "family energy" on doing things for the kids, he says, which leaves little or no time left for the marriage.

"Family" starts with marriage. Your marriage, if it's a good one, will be with you longer than your children will. Marriage is lifelong. Parenting is self-limiting by nature. Put your husband and his needs first.

This is hard for some people to do, especially when the children are small. Infant and toddler needs are immediate; husbands can wait. But there is a difference between immediacy and importance. If your baby won't tolerate a sitter and your marriage desperately needs some personal time together, leave the baby with the sitter. Infants will survive their fear of strangers; a strained marriage may not survive neglect.

Is there such a thing as a modern low-stress marriage? Yes, there *are* marriages that thrive on little dissension and much affirming and agreement. They are lived by people who work at their marriage daily in many small ways to build closeness.

Psychologist John Gottmann, marriage specialist and author of *Why Marriages Succeed or Fail,* says that connecting on small things of low emotional intensity is the single most effective way to build a satisfying marriage. Show interest in what your partner is saying and doing, he advises. Ask, "How did it go today?" Share your joys. Celebrate each other's raises and promotions. Accept and respect your partner's feelings, even if you don't agree with them. And, when your marriage partner is upset, listen without becoming defensive or giving unsolicited advice.

Express frequently your appreciation of the person your husband is and tell him how proud you are of the things he does. Call, or ask him to call you, if one of you is traveling out of town for more than a day or two. Hold hands. Hug. Do this in private if public displays of affection bother either of you. Joke around and tease each other.

Get physical. Ten seconds spent resting a hand on your husband's arm, eyes meeting, while sipping coffee together before the kids get up will cast a glow over your whole day, and his. It may even last for weeks. Shared personal moments are that memorable.

Though these little acts sound trivial, bunched together they spell love and respect—the two things people want and need most from marriage, Gottmann says.

Modern couples often find little time for sexual intimacy. Take time. Sexual intercourse is the deepest, most lasting, and most meaningful expression of the emotional bond between the two of you. If you don't enjoy your sex life, get help. You need this spiritual treasure, especially in the climate surrounding today's fast-paced lifestyles.

Low-stress Parenting

In raising your children, avoid today's popular overkill. Stop studying and analyzing every little parenting responsibility or difficulty. Modern psychology has helped society unearth many causes of problem behaviors, but most families fall within a norm that functions well. The children in these families are thriving, content, and happy. If yours are not, professional counseling will give you better results than self-counseling will.

Parenting is not as difficult as our culture suggests. It is a challenge that takes much patience and energy, but it need not be hard mental exercise. Regardless of parenting style, all but the most troubled children will generally thrive on parenting that is based on common sense, consistency in applying the rules, love, and sincere attempts at understanding.

If you care about your children, it will come through. If you try to understand what it must be like to be a three-year-old who suddenly has to share Mommy and Daddy with a new baby brother, you will expect your toddler to show some jealousy. If you yourself were raised in a happy home, you had good role models for raising children. If you were not, there are many books and classes available today to assist you.

Instead of worrying about your parenting skills, why not spend this time and energy toward having positive work and play experiences with your children? This gives your family more opportunities to enjoy one another's company. Today's busy families have enough trouble trying to find enough time just for that.

Expect your children to do things for themselves as much as they can. It's better for them as well as you. My children made their own school lunches from the time they started school. Not only did this eliminate complaints about the contents of their lunchboxes, but it also saved precious early-morning time for someone who doesn't do well in the early mornings. Best of all, they never minded.

If you are married, expect your husband to help with child

raising. Children need fathering as well as mothering. Parenting requires vast amounts of physical energy when the children are small, and lots of emotional energy when they are older.

Even teenagers need a parent around. My greatest childhood crisis came in ninth grade when I lost a new "best friend" to a move a few months after enrolling in a new and strange high school. My support system was gone at a time when I badly needed one. Fortunately my mother was around to assure me I would soon be making new friends.

The parenting should be shared according to the relative needs of each of you on that particular day. If you have been working overtime all week doing the annual inventory at your plant, let your husband take over. If he is overly stressed from the threat of a strike at his company, you do the honors. Respond jointly when the demand calls for it. If your teenager is defying his grounding, stand together and insist he honor the house rules.

Single parents have a much greater challenge in meeting the demands of parenting, especially if the absent parent is not closely and regularly involved in the children's lives. Single parents may need to forego working overtime or indulging many of their personal interests until the children are old enough to manage for themselves.

Because the parenting demands are so heavy for single parents, those who carry this role need all the more to have a viable and healthy personal life, away from the steady twenty-four-hours-a-day, seven-days-a-week responsibility. Not only will this time away reduce your stress, but also you will be a better parent when you are "on duty."

To lower your parenting stress quota, limit your children's involvements. Today's parents think they must provide every opportunity available to develop their children's talents and pursue their interests. Too often this means the parents are constantly running children to and from ball games, play rehearsals, Scout meetings, and the like. This leaves little time for the child to experience some free time (sadly neglected today), and there is less time for the family to enjoy one another's company or for the parents to pursue their own interests.

One way to solve this dilemma is to have children prioritize their activities. Allow one music, sports, or recreational activity (dance, drama, or whatever) per child at a time plus church group or Scouts. If a child has multiple interests, let the child try something different when the sessions change, over summer vacation, or when the new school year starts. Many parents keep their children super-busy, hoping this will encourage them to stay off drugs and out of gangs. This can be counter-productive. Family-life experts tell us that the most effective means to that end is confident parenting and a strong, healthy family life.

Finding Together Time

"The best inheritance a parent can give his children is a few minutes of his time each day," said O. A. Battista. As a general rule, children don't need much. A mere two minutes spent one-on-one tucking a child into bed and talking about how things went at school that day is worth diamonds. Quality time like this is precious because it tells your child that he or she is very important in your life. All the quantity time in the world holds minimal value if the quality ingredient is missing. If a mom stays home with her kids day and night, but spends all of this time doing housework, talking with friends on the phone, reading romance novels, and watching television, there is not a great deal of value in her being there for the children.

Is quantity time important? Yes, to some extent. Researchers say the key to a family's strength and happiness is the degree of emotional closeness between family members. Are your child's emotional needs being met in the amount of time you, or you and your husband, are spending with the child? Thom Hunter, author of *Those Not-So-Still Small Voices*, says the thing he missed most about not having a daddy was his father's "not being there" for the events that bind father to son—such things as the school picnic, ball games, and watching the eggs hatch in the bird's nest on the front porch.

Be sensitive to the emotional needs of each of your children. If one starts "acting out," you'll know something is wrong. A number of years ago, my husband began taking short travel jaunts for his company. We had only had our adopted son a few years. Kenny became temperamental and started scrapping frequently with his sisters. He thought his new father was abandoning him, as he felt his first family had. Peter intentionally stopped traveling, and Kenny settled down shortly thereafter.

In the frantic pace of today's world, it may be difficult to find sufficient quantity time. A chaplain I once knew had a good policy. He recorded on his weekly calendar as many appointments to spend time with his family as he did with the people that he called on in prisons and hospitals. That meant devoting two weekday nights every week to his home life. "My children and wife need me as much as my clients do," he said.

Ralph Keyes in *Timelock* tells of a Kansas family that made lists of things each person loved and hated to do. They found that the father hated overtime work, the mother didn't enjoy her many community activities, and their son preferred working with plants to playing on his soccer team. On the other side of the ledger, they all loved camping and taking walks. So the son quit soccer, the parents cut back on their commitments, and the family started taking more walks and doing more camping.

One of the most rewarding ways to bond as a family is to make dinnertime a family affair. Have each member of your family share his or her day—the frustrations, silly happenings, positive and negative moments, and new discoveries. Mealtimes are often the only time busy families have available to engage in stimulating conversation. They are also an ideal time to get better acquainted with one another's emotional needs and to teach ethics and good behavior: "What do all of you think Josh should have done when his locker partner broke his science project?"

If you can't arrange a relaxed meal together every night, try for once or twice a week. Sometimes is better than never. Turn off the television; it is a distraction, and it isolates people. Also, don't let this time degenerate into a battleground or a correction session. Social worker Michael Abrahams advises, "How mealtime is used—to argue or converse, discipline or praise—is a good barometer of whether a family is drifting apart or drawing closer." This is a time to support and bring out the best in each other. If the children stray from that objective, pull them gently but firmly back on track. Another good way to build precious family ties is to carry out one or more challenging family projects. This could be a vegetable garden in the summer, a musical ensemble, or an ongoing family photo album. It could be regular from-scratch baking sessions or building a sailboat. The key is to find a project everyone enjoys working on.

Problems Scheduling Family Time

It is hard for many working women to get their employers to honor their commitments to their families. Dr. Klein found in his study that the average "family friendliness" score of 118 Fortune 1000 companies was only 68 out of a possible 610 points. "It is not unusual for working parents to have to tell their bosses they can't work late or on a weekend because of [family] responsibilities," says Paula Ancona, who writes the newspaper column, "Working Smarter."

To offset this, Ancona suggests that you talk at work about your family so the company recognizes your dedication to them. Ask your boss to give you adequate notice when you may have to work late, and discuss together how and to what extent you could accommodate such a request. Approach the matter as a business problem, not your request for a favor.

Seek creative solutions to child-care emergencies. (Could you bring your child to work or do the work at home?) If you have to leave work early for a family event, give your boss as much notice as possible and be honest about your reason for leaving. Ask if arrangements could be made at the office to get your work done by someone else. Also, seek support from other employees with similar family-minded concerns.

Things can get hectic in the "working mom" family. Bathrooms get overcrowded in the morning. If you are married, who takes off work when one of the children gets sick? Many families have to cope with the ongoing need to hire and retain a capable, dependable sitter for the children. Vacations have to be coordinated. So do the varying schedules of all family members.

Here are some tips that might help:

Post a family calendar on the refrigerator and record everyone's commitments—business and personal—on it.

To solve insufficient bathroom space, *establish a bathroom time schedule.* Write it out, if necessary. If that doesn't solve the problem, have some family members shower the night before.

If married, *share the "sick child" duties* as your jobs and benefits allow. Does one have more personal time than the other? Can one get away more readily?

Schedule your vacations for when you can all be together. If that does not work, plan an at-home or nearby vacation, so the missing family member can join you when he or she can.

Sitters are the major worry for caring parents. Have a backup plan—a neighbor, perhaps—and place your priorities on obtaining a loving person or agency, even if it costs a bit more. You will be considerably less stressed if you do not have to worry about what is going on at the sitter's while you work.

Share the Care of Elderly Parents

Many families are concerned with the care of elderly parents. Statistics show that women end up being the primary caregiver in these situations. Caring for the special needs of the elderly takes time and patience and is emotionally draining. It is heart-wrenching to visit your mother or grandmother week after week, only to have her look into your eyes blankly and ask, "Who are you?"

The multiple roles many women must play leave them feeling pulled in many directions. Caregivers need rest, relief, and support. Look for ways within your family and the community to obtain help. Most larger cities today have multiple types of services available—day care, respite care, visiting nurse services, and the like. Discuss with your parent's physician appropriate options.

Family members can help, too. Children have a special rapport with the elderly; let yours share time with Grandma. Teenage and adult children can run errands for her. Have your siblings share the care of Mom and her possessions. Seek support from the appropriate caregiver support group: the stroke club, Alzheimer's support group, or whatever group is designed to meet your particular needs.

"Shall we put Mom in a home?" is a difficult and stressful decision. All options should be considered seriously. Family members should not be expected to take on the responsibility of caring for her in their home if they don't feel they can manage it; this has to be an honest, individual decision. Do not feel guilty if the answer to the question above is yes. This is a dilemma all families of the elderly face today. The problems go far beyond having enough time and energy for the care of the parent.

As with all of life's tough decisions, praying for God's direction provides maximum stress relief.

14

De-stress Your Family and Other Relationships

"We cannot make people over. Our business is to make ourselves better and others happy, and this is enough to keep us busy."
——Joseph Fort Newton in *The Atlantic*

To build strong relationships and minimize the chance of stressful conflict, we need to accept people as they are. We must let them be the persons God created them to be and that they want to be. To do any less is to deny them God's full destiny for them.

This is not easy as it sounds. We can't help wishing our husbands and children would fulfill some of our needs and our desires for them. We would like coworkers to do things our way because it looks easier to us and is more comfortable for us to work with.

That is not God's way. Nor does it work. Trying to change others into what *we* want results in futility and frustration for us and provokes hostility from them. The challenge is for us to accept others rather than expect them to mold themselves to our vision for them.

Accept Other People

Allow your husband to be himself. You married him in part because he had a personality that differs from yours—one that attracted you. Enjoy the richness your differences bring to your relationship. My husband is casual and likes country music. I am semi-traditional and like popular classics and contemporary gospel. His favorite volunteer project is driving the pickup truck for a local food pantry. Mine is singing in the church choir. He goes to my events as often as he is able, and I go to his. We enjoy the challenge of blending our tastes and sharing the stories that emerge from our differing interests.

Men's thinking patterns and conversational style differ from women's. That makes it hard to understand where your husband is coming from at times. Deborah Tannen illuminates many of those differences in *You Just Don't Understand.* Men seek status, while women seek support, she says. Men seek independence, women seek intimacy. To men, talk is information; to women, talk is an attempt to verbalize their feelings. Try to check out why your husband responds as he does to things. Ask him to restate his thinking. A clearer understanding not only relieves tension and corrects misunderstandings, but it also broadens your own view.

Let your children be themselves. Many parents today overemphasize grades and push college to ensure that their children will be able to earn a good living. This is not a good idea. The child who wants to go to college won't need to be pushed, and you cannot make a scholastic genius out of a child whose gifts lean more towards gymnastics or mechanics. Nor can you make your demure child into an assertive, shining star. Save yourself and your child a lot of stress. Do what is best for the child, not your dreams for your child.

Accept your children on their level. You'll frustrate your child and yourself if you expect your three-year-old to hang up his jacket every time he comes into the house. You'll be living in an armed camp if you expect your fourteen-year-old to act like a responsible twenty-year-old.

Stepmothers, accept the children of your husband's prior

marriage. They are dear to him. And be tolerant of the many ways the turmoil that surrounds their young lives rubs off onto yours. *"My* mom lets me do it *this* way," can be turned around with: "That's a very good way, but your dad and I do it differently here, Julie." "I don't *like* you!" can generate a soft "That's okay, Julie. But your daddy does, and that is what matters." Try to accept your stepchildren's mother. You both share something very special—the children.

At work or when doing volunteer or other services, be open to other people's work habits. Someone else's way may be harder for you than yours, or it might be easier. It may be more difficult but might produce better results. Keep an open mind, try it, and see what you can learn. You can always go back to your way.

Search for other people's areas of strength and compliment them on these. When you work together, build on these strengths. You can always learn something from other people. And, when you work with them and praise their talents, they are more open to recognize and work with yours.

Be Reasonable in Your Expectations

If your husband wants to hang on to his beatup recliner in the living room, let him. It's his house, too. It is more important that he be happy in his home than that your house be a showcase for *House Beautiful*.

Laid-back people tend to marry industrious people. These are the best kinds of marriages because the spouses compensate for each other's bent. Unfortunately this opposing characteristic can rub the other spouse raw from time to time. A marriage counselor friend once told me that people often divorce for the same reason they marry.

Mend, don't *end* the marriage when these rough edges show up. Tolerate eighty percent of them and resolve the rest. Experts concur that disagreements will arise in any marriage. The ability to disagree without hurting each other measures the soundness of a relationship. A good marriage brings out the best in us, despite—or possibly even because of—our differences and conflicts.

Love and let be. We're all human. We all irritate and annoy each other from time to time. We all are impossible to live with at times. So live by the Golden Rule. Jesus said, "In everything do to others as you would have them do to you" (Matthew 7:12). If you want your husband to accept you as the person you are and to forgive your bad days, do the same for him.

Be reasonable in your expectations of your children. If your toddler spills his milk, say "Oh, oh!" and cheerfully wipe it up. All children are clumsy before they are capable. Most of them tell a whopper of a lie and cut their own hair at least once in the process of growing up. Expect these things to happen. Teach when they do; don't scold.

With adults, live and let live. Live your life and let others live theirs—without interference, manipulation, or control from you. Refrain from giving advice to a teen or other adult unless that person asks for it. Advice does no good unless and until the hearers are in a frame of mind to accept what they hear. Pushing your point comes across to others as unwanted control. When your adult son buys a car he can't afford, let him. It is his right. He may burn himself financially, but he'll survive. And he'll learn better that way. If your husband wants to spend his Saturdays on the golf course instead of helping with chores at home, maybe he needs the relaxation. Work your plans for sharing the at-home workload around his indulgence. He'll love you for it.

Avoid telling coworkers or friends how to do things (that is, your way). Your way may not work for them. Also, stifle the urge to tell them how to solve their problems. They have to find their own way on that path too.

De-stress Your Parenting Role

It is less stressful for the whole family when parents require courtesy, respect, and good behavior from their children. Though these qualities are not promoted well by society these days, they are God's will for your children, and they make life easier both for you and for them. Children need to learn to obey. In fact, all people do. Not even adults are free

116

to do as they choose. We all have to follow the laws of society, and as Christians the will of our Maker. Children learn it best if they learn early how to respect the rights of other people—including their parents.

Concentrate your teaching on good habits and sound values. Tell your children what they are doing right. When they do something wrong, teach them the correct way. Don't preach. You'll have greater success and less stress.

Jeremy shoplifted a pack of gum. Rather than scold, his mother explained to Jeremy what "ownership" means—having something as a gift or by purchase, not by taking. Together they went back to the store, where Jeremy apologized for his mistake and paid for the gum from his allowance.

Teaching values is vital today. In a Girl Scout Survey on Beliefs and Moral Values, sixty-five percent of America's high school students said they would cheat on an important exam. Fifty-three percent said they would lie to protect a friend who vandalized school property. This is the world your children are growing up in. Use every opportunity you can find to impress God's value system on them.

Rivalry among both siblings and stepsiblings is trying at times to the most patient of parents. Home is a training ground where children learn how to hold their own in the world. The rivalry is a jousting to try out different lances. Teach your children basic social rules such as taking turns, fair play, and tolerance of differences. Accept the jousting as vital to acquiring the skills needed to implement these rules. Step in only when a child misunderstands or misapplies the rules—bullying, teasing unmercifully, or the like.

Problems arise frequently between parents and their stepchildren. Older children especially are often hostile to a stepparent. Experts suggest that discipline in these cases be left to the natural parent. This is good advice to a point because it is often the only way that works. But both parents must agree on the house rules, and the rules must be applied equally to all children in the household. Children can handle two sets of rules, but they cannot handle partiality or unfairness. Nor should they be asked to. Also, for order and harmony in the household, stepparents must have the right to steer all parties aboard the ship in the absence of the natural parent.

Rebellious defiance is troublesome for most parents. The most effective and least stressful method of handling disciplinary infractions is to apply appropriate, prompt, and certain punishment. Some children are by nature more rebellious than others. Be tolerant and loving but firm with these children. This is easier to come by if you tell yourself, "Someday this child may need a lot of feistiness to stand up for what he (or she) believes in. That makes this a good quality to have."

Let Others Do Things Their Way

When it comes to sharing family errands or chores, let your husband and children do them their own way. It may not be your way or to your liking, but what matters is that they are participating in the work of living.

When my depression hit years ago, a family friend offered me her help. My house was a disaster zone, what with three small children running around and a heavy schedule of work I had let go for the sake of my anemia and numerous trips to the doctor with little Susie. What would lighten my load the most, I told my friend, was to have my house cleaned. She did so, but not in the way I would have done it. She missed the oven—one of my most annoying hot spots—and dusted places I never worried about. This bothered me. I was ungrateful. I was also wrong. The house was cleaner for the children and much more presentable for guests who stopped by. She did me good service—her way. Let your family members give one another good service—their way.

I am not suggesting here that parents tolerate deliberate slipshod efforts by recalcitrant children. It is important to have minimum standards and expect that they be followed. Good workmanship is a character quality all children need to acquire.

For happier family relationships, restrict chores to what is reasonable and common. It is unfair to family members to ask them to tend to others' personal projects that require extraordinary effort. Mom may treasure her knick-knack shelf, but she should not expect other family members to keep it dusted for her. If Dad wants an elaborate perennial garden, the children should not have to keep it weeded every week for him. If family members *want* to help with such projects, this is fine, but their participation should be voluntary.

The same principle can be applied conversely to personal interests that bother the rest of the family. Family members should not have to stumble over daughter Desiree's favorite beanbag chair because she likes it plopped in the middle of the room for watching television. Son David should not be allowed to squeal the tires on his car, sending out screeches that startle the whole neighborhood.

Communicate

To better understand one another, family members need to keep in touch with one another's plans, expectations, dreams, and goals. The family calendar can lay out events but cannot tell the rest of the family how worried Mark is about doing well in cross country. The family may be more tolerant of Mom's crankiness if they know she is working against a tight deadline at the office.

Adequate communication is vital to the emotional closeness that makes family living great. Husbands and wives need to try to touch base daily: "How did your meeting go today?" If the children can join in on this, so much the better. Often schedules, especially in larger families, are too frantic. Weekends are often a good time to pick up the pieces at a family sharing or conference time.

For stronger family ties, encourage your family to be a support system for one another at dinner or these other family conference times. Ideally, when the children are grown, family members will change their roles from parent-child and sibling-sibling to one of friendship with each other. Though siblings will vary in their closeness to each other, some good groundwork for the future can be laid at these talk sessions.

Can the whole family attend Sharon's swim meet and Danny's Little League game? Probably not. But encourage those who can to attend. It means a great deal. I once mentored a confirmation student in my church who was playing on a city league baseball team. I surprised her one day by showing up for a game. No one from her family had been able to make it. She grinned when she saw me and told me she appreciated having a fan club. None of us ever gets too many of these little touches of love.

Agree to disagree. In healthy families, all family members have the right to express their own opinions—outrageous ones included. If six-year-old Josh thinks our nation should go to war over a trifle, accept his thinking as a sincere and desirable interest in what his country is doing. Children that young can't be expected to show sound judgment. If your teen challenges church teachings about sex, he may not be losing his values but merely parroting what he hears from friends. Ask, "Do you think that is a good idea? Do you think it works well?" Urge him to seek his own answers according to his faith and values, not those of others.

The Bible assures us that if we bring up our children in the nurture and admonition of the Lord they will not depart from it in the long run. In the short run, we cannot prevent them from making some mistakes. But that will occur whether we try to prevent them or not. They are less apt to err if we bring them up right and then trust them to follow God's ways.

Small family problems, such as which of the family's three cars will be stored in the two-car garage, can be handled at these family councils. Save internal family conflicts for another time. They need to be addressed, and in good time, but family sharing sessions do not provide the proper atmosphere. Disputes are best settled when given their own time, an appropriate place, and adequate space.

Build Bonds

Build strong family ties by working together. Where possible, schedule two persons for family chores. If two siblings scrap constantly (as my two youngest always did), schedule

Mom or Dad with one of the children to unload the dishwasher and put everything away.

Build bonds by playing together. Even a quick ten minutes playing catch in the backyard has immense love value.

Study together. My husband took an auto repair class with our single-parent daughter at a local technical school. She likes being able to troubleshoot her car problems herself, as does he. They shared a special interest while strengthening cherished ties.

Worship and pray together. There is a third party in every Christian marriage and an extra guest at the table in every Christian household. The abundant blessing that comes with sharing one faith and the constant presence of our Lord in our lives cannot be underestimated. God is our Father, and Christ the unseen brother who undergirds our struggles to live wisely and well. "Underneath are the everlasting arms" (Deuteronomy 33:27, RSV) that expand the richness, fill the voids, and uphold us through all the troubles in our lives. The shared faith of a family enables family members to enjoy each other more and support one another better when life's reverses come.

Laugh and celebrate together. Fun and family traditions built on the concrete foundation of Christian family living enrich our lives enormously. On our recent trip to Mexico, Peter and I traveled through many small villages. The whole tour group noticed that these people appeared to be happier than those we ran across in the large cities. Their lives were built around the church, an abundant extended family and community life, and the shared burden of helping one another in times of misfortune. Our families can do the same in our lives.

Quiz

How strong are your family attitudes and relationships? Let's check.

___ My husband and children come ahead of my job.

___ My husband and I discuss our wants and needs with each other at least once a week.

121

___ My husband and I talk over our day nearly every day.

___ I thank or compliment him almost every day.

___ I feel comfortable with my style of parenting.

___ My children feel comfortable with my parenting most of the time.

___ My children usually obey me and are respectful and well behaved.

___ I have many positive experiences with my children.

___ Our family spends time together daily or almost daily.

___ Our family works, plays, and worships together.

___ Our family enjoys one another's company, for the most part.

___ My family shares the care of our frail elderly family members.

___ I pray for my family, including our elderly parent(s), daily.

15

Defuse Conflicts Quickly and Lovingly

Sally looked sadly around the Christmas dinner table at her three sons and their families. One family was missing—that of her youngest son, Tim. Five years earlier, Tim had asked his closest brother to stand up at his wedding. The eldest brother was miffed and would not attend. Tim was so hurt, he refused to speak to this brother or attend any family events where he was present. Neither would take the first step toward reconciliation.

Conflict drains emotional energies. If the conflict is a grave one, the wounds run deep. Conflict keeps us from doing our work well, enjoying our family life, and getting the most from life. Serious family conflicts stress all family members.

Because we are human, some conflict is certain to arise. Communication is not a perfect art, nor are people perfect. The closer we are to other people, the more likely we are to step on each other's feet. Not only do we miscommunicate, but we also misbehave at times.

Conflicts need not destroy the serenity of our lives. Now that behavioral psychology has made so many inroads to better understanding ourselves and others, we can learn how to identify the source of relational problems and respond in ways that heal rather than inflict deeper cuts.

Defusing Minor Conflicts

When minor conflicts arise, let them go. If your two-year-old slaps your face, gently push her hand aside with the admonition, "That is not the right way to say no, Alicia. If you don't like what Mommy said, say 'I don't like that!' and we'll talk about it." Little ones don't know a slap is a personal offense, nor do they know how to express their anger in acceptable ways. When your teenager objects to house rules, commend his desire to be independent and clarify that house rules are not a negotiable item, whereas his choice of clothing or curfew might be.

Tolerate a lot from people with whom you don't interact constantly. Our neighbor wanted to build a new fence where we had a preexisting one. I asked him to discuss it with me before he went ahead with his plans, as the fence backed a treasured flower border in view of my kitchen window. One day his contractor began erecting the new fence behind my older one, ruining the overall appearance. Immediately I cut mine down, as his was an attractive alternative. The neighbor later apologized, explaining that he planned to talk with me, but the contractor showed up one morning earlier than expected. Even had he not acted in good faith, the situation did not warrant a neighborly dispute.

When You Can't Let Things Go . . .

Sometimes we can't let things go. Some words, incidents, and situations affect us too deeply to let them pass. If you cannot put a troubling situation behind you, confront the person as promptly as you are able. Hanging on to these kinds of problems encourages resentment to build.

Try to work things out in nonadversarial, loving ways. Today we know conflicts can be resolved quickly in quiet, peaceful ways—bringing richness, closeness, and a depth to the relationship that wasn't there before. The love between these persons then blossoms with lovelier fragrance and greater fullness. The following guidelines show how.

1. *Pick a good time and place to talk.* Talking things over

is emotionally draining. It needs a welcoming climate—one conducive to calm, unhurried conversation. So avoid complaining about anything the minute your spouse comes in the door after work. Or when he has a headache. Or if one of the kids just splattered pizza on the carpet. Instead, tell your partner or child you would like to talk later. Set a time when things will be more serene (but make it soon); then put a hold on the matter until that time.

Similarly, don't discuss a problem when you yourself are under pressure or at your grouchy time of the day. Years ago I frequently spat out sarcastic digs in the early morning. Eventually I found that, if I waited to discuss troublesome matters until after I drank two cups of coffee, I was more controlled and polite.

Since most conflict results from power struggles, "turf" is important. England's Queen Victoria and her beloved Prince Albert got into a tiff one day shortly after they married. Albert stalked out of the room and locked himself in his private apartments. Victoria hammered furiously on his door.

"Who's there?" Albert asked.

"The queen of England, and she demands to be admitted."

Albert did not respond, and the door remained locked.

Victoria hammered again.

"Who's there?" Albert said.

"The queen . . . and she demands . . ." The door stayed shut.

Victoria paused, then tapped gently. To his, "Who's there?" she replied, "Your wife, Albert." The prince immediately opened the door.

Neutral turf levels the playing field. If your teenager "wants to be treated like an adult," take a walk together or sit down with colas at a nearby restaurant.

Don't allow interruptions, if you can help it. With a spousal conflict, you may want to wait until the children are in bed. If they are older, send them to their rooms a bit early (No, it really *doesn't* hurt them). And turn on the telephone answering machine.

Don't try to work things out if you are depressed or in pain.

Wait until you feel better. As a chronic arthritic I discovered years ago that when I am hurting, small problems loom monstrous. When the pain is gone, problems are not nearly as bad as they seemed.

Sometimes matters *MUST* be discussed immediately. If so, put aside all else and tend to it.

2. *State your case briefly and clearly.* Tell the other person how you view the situation. Be direct. Don't beat around the bush. "This is what happened, as I see it."

Handle one problem at a time—the most pressing concern first—and be specific: "You did (or did not) do _____." Avoid bringing up old charges that should have been dealt with days or months ago. Let them go; they are past history. What matters is what happened on this occasion. And don't generalize ("You always do that"). Generalizations only muddy the waters.

3. *Attack the PROBLEM, not the person.* In stating your case, explain, don't condemn. Your goal is to maintain a good relationship. It defeats the purpose to tear down the other person. It demeans another to say, "You were an insensitive clod last night. You forgot to take out the garbage." Your partner's dignity is preserved and tempers will remain cooler if you put it this way: "Because you forgot to take out the garbage, I walked into a stinky kitchen this morning. It actually gave me a headache to walk into that room."

4. *Describe your feelings about what happened.* To resolve conflicts lovingly, we need to listen to and deal with each other's feelings. That is not easy. Feelings tell better than words what people really want. But because we find it hard to focus on and identify our feelings, our thoughts often don't match our feelings. That really confuses us, for we don't know which we should listen to.

Even when we do recognize our feelings, it is often difficult to put them into words. Use the "I" method. Tell how you felt about what happened: "I was disappointed. I was depending on you to take care of the garbage."

5. *Listen to the other person.* Keep an open mind. Try to see yourself through his or her eyes by asking yourself, How

126

would I feel in such a situation? Usually, you will feel a kinship with that person's viewpoint. To her husband's, "I'm sorry, honey. I just forgot!" an honest listener would have to reply, "I can relate to that. I've forgotten things, too."

If you cannot relate to the other person's feelings, be broad-minded. Each person has a right to view things his or her own way. Our thinking is colored by the different backgrounds we bring to the life situations we encounter. "Do not judge, so that you may not be judged," Jesus advises us (Matt. 7:1).

Sometimes we find upon closer scrutiny that the other person is right. If so, admit it and apologize. In instances where you cannot come to a mutual understanding, bear in mind that what is wrong for you might still be right for the other person.

6. *Play fair.* Be aboveboard in your dealings. Don't go behind a person's back and build enemy support: "Kids, your dad didn't do his chores!" Respect the person's right to privacy. Similarly, avoid discussing personal problems in front of uninvolved persons. Airing the family's dirty laundry makes everyone uneasy. Value privacy as a gift you give each other.

7. *Accept responsibility for what YOU contributed to the problem.* Every party supplies *something* to any given conflict, even if it is nothing more than harboring unreasonable expectations. Identify where you have contributed to the problem and own up to it: "Everybody forgets sometimes. I was too quick to complain. I should have been more understanding."

Sometimes we bait other persons into altercations. If a wife "orders" instead of "asks" her husband to take out the garbage, she is treating him like a servant and thus welcoming trouble. Any time we demean another human being with our words or actions, we are baiting.

8. *Apologize.* We can and should apologize for any trouble we caused and for whatever we have contributed to a given problem. But sometimes trouble just happens and it isn't anybody's fault. Children spill milk because they are awkward. People bump into others because they lose their balance.

Here again, apologize. Apologizing doesn't always mean that you are responsible for the problem. It simply means you regret what happened. It shows you care. However, don't apologize for something you did not do, just to "keep the peace." Insincerity and capitulation do not build sound, healthy relationships. They come off as condescending. The family member or friend with whom you are in conflict wants to be respected and to respect you. Therefore this person needs truthfulness about your involvement in the fracas. The idea is to strive for healthy balance.

9. *Forgive and forget.* When other people have wronged you and sincerely regret it, forgive fully and forget promptly.

This is not always simple—especially the forgetting. The latter is vitally important because it completes the circle to restoring good will in the relationship, and the relationship is what counts. Not just forgiving but forgetting as well is also God's will for human relationships: "Godly grief produces a repentance that leads to salvation *and brings no regret*" (2 Cor. 7:10).

People can't forgive others just by willing it to happen. The method that works for me personally is to try to understand *why* the person did what he or she did, and then accept the person's right to do it, even though in my eyes it was a mistake.

Ultimately, the best way to forgive and forget is to follow Jesus' advice: "First take the log out of your own eye, and then you will see clearly to take the speck out of your neighbor's eye" (Matt. 7:4-5). We all let other people down, in big ways at times. Jesus asked us to forgive others, just as we want God and other people to forgive us our human frailties.

10. *Ask for what you want.* Once a problem has been aired from both perspectives, move towards a solution. State that you want to work things out, and tell why. This affirms your intent to hold the relationship uppermost. "I know this is just a little thing, honey, but we have so much going for us in our marriage. I have always been able to depend on you. I don't want anything to spoil that."

Give the other person time and space, as needed. We come

to terms with ordeals at different rates of speed and in our own ways. True caring does not crowd the other person. George got into a heated argument with his brother, Hank, after Hank mishandled their parents' estate. Hank knew he had done wrong, but he was extremely proud, never able to admit his mistakes. Eventually they came to a workable relationship again, but only after each allowed the other enough time and space to heal the hurts inflicted.

When a Conflict Cannot Be Easily Resolved

If things can't be worked out, try the Lord's method. Sit down together with an impartial third party in whom both of you have confidence, and ask this person's advice. If that does not work, try professional counseling. If the other person refuses to try to work things out and you are struggling to cope, get counseling for yourself.

Divorce is sometimes the only answer in marital disputes. Christ himself recognized that when He gave reluctant consent to it (Matt. 5:31-32). But divorce is neither an easy answer nor a good out. Separation for a time while working on the problems often works better for all concerned parties. If the problems that gave rise to the divorce are not recognized and resolved, later marriages will also fail. Divorces are costly. They reduce substantially the economic status of both parties. Children of divorce are usually torn by their love for both parents. Divorce is justifiable, but only when it is the lesser of two evils and all other avenues to heal the rift have been exhausted.

Let your children settle their own disputes, where possible. They might surprise you, as mine once did. When my older two daughters were four and six, my husband's boss gave them a cigar band (paper ring) one day to play with. Only one ring for two little people. That spells trouble, for sure. Not knowing quite what to do, I let them work it out. They did. One would get it first, for five minutes. When the other one's turn came, she got to wear it for ten. Because of the bonus, they had no difficulty settling on who came first.

When your older children cannot resolve a conflict, step

in as soon as you see things start to escalate. Don't play favorites. Seat them face to face, and let each state his or her case without interruption. Repeat the story each one tells, using your own words. This clarifies what that person is trying to say.

When both have finished, recall some good times the two have shared. This reminds them they are capable of enjoying each other's company. Finally, ask each one what he or she wants of the other, and ask the opposing party for consent. Keep going until both sides have found acceptable ground.

You can also use these guidelines if you are called on to intervene in an interfamily dispute, but don't get involved unless you are asked to by the parties involved. You may make matters worse or end up with both parties being angry with you.

Nonfamily Conflicts

If you are in conflict with a coworker, follow these same procedures. If the conflict cannot be worked out, take it to your boss. If your boss will not help you resolve it, ask if you can get remediation through your employee assistance program.

If all efforts fail, you may want to consider looking for another position, even if it means less pay. Your health is more important than your present job or salary. Severe, long-lasting relationship difficulties will sooner or later affect your health.

If you have a conflict with someone you don't have to work with closely or directly (a neighbor or relative, for instance), stay open but distance yourself from that person until he or she wants to work things out. Accept the fact that the matter may never be resolved. Some people choose to have an antagonistic spirit.

Adult sibling conflicts often arise, especially when it comes time to settle family estates. If you are in conflict with a brother or sister, try to work out the problems. If the other person shows no interest in ending the difficulty, walk away. Life is too short to dwell on or hang onto family disputes.

A man inherited one tenth of his parents' farm. Two of his brothers refused to sell the farm or to pay off in cash the other heirs. Family wars raged for months, then years. Exasperated and disheartened, the man finally donated his share to the local church. End of stress.

Quiz

How good are your conflict resolution skills? Answer Y for yes, N for no.

___ A loving relationship is more important to me than being right.

___ I would rather let little troubles go than fight them out.

___ When I am steamed, I can wait to talk things over. I don't have to have satisfaction now!

___ I listen well.

___ When resolving a conflict, I don't discuss the other person's faults, only the problem between us.

___ I don't ask outsiders to back up my arguments.

___ I always look for what I might have done to cause or contribute to a given problem.

___ I forgive readily.

___ When I forgive, I forget about what happened and don't bring it up again.

Ways to Settle Conflicts

When settling differences that require action, look for creative options. Contrary to popular thinking, compromise is not the only, nor is it necessarily the best, way to go. Compromise usually means both parties end up sacrificing something. Here are some good alternative options:

- Do it together.
- Take turns. Try one person's way first, then the other.

- Leave the outcome to chance. Flip a coin.
- Find common ground. Settle on something both of you would like to do (or buy, or whatever).
- Give in. This works well when one party feels strongly about something and the other does not. In using it, explore the intensity of each other's feelings. If the option of giving in is used correctly, the aftereffects are surprisingly gratifying.
- Arbitrate. Get a respected outsider's opinion.
- Avoid a settlement. Agree to disagree.

Some of these options are good only for minor problems. Some carry built-in limitations (you cannot always find common ground). Not all are workable in all situations. But with many of them the parties involved gain more and sacrifice less than with compromise.

You may have alternatives not listed here. If you think they will evoke a loving response, try them.

16

Simplify Meals and Mealtimes

One day a number of years ago I felt bogged down about how much time I was spending on nonwriting activities. Since food service was such a big part of my day, I took time to figure out how much time on the average I was spending grocery shopping, cooking and baking, serving, eating, and cleaning up after our daily meals. It was an astounding four hours. That's half a work day! It is also half of the customary allotment of personal and family time that most full-time working women have available to them on weekday nights. No wonder we are so rushed and stressed!

For ease of living (and to teach independent living skills and encourage responsibility) spread around the duties surrounding meal service—menu planning, shopping, cooking, table setting, and cleanup. Even pint-size family members can help, and they like to—usually more than the older children do.

Start by simplifying the meals themselves.

Easy Menu Planning

Meal planning can be a trial. It not only takes time, but it also requires ingenuity if you like variety and excitement in your menus. A quick pizza thrown in the oven is so much easier! But you can serve a variety of nutritious delectable meals and still hold preparation time to a minimum. A number of cookbooks now on the market enable you to do just that. Most of them revolve around the same concept, the one I use most often—the one-pot meal.

For ease of menu planning, compile a recipe file or other list of quick-and-easy meals your family likes. Stir-frys are especially appetizing, but microwaved and broiled meals are also quick. The variety of sources for one-pots is endless, as all ethnic groups seem to use them. I file mine by meat, poultry, fish, and meatless entrees (beans, cheese, and egg main dishes).

As a general planning guide for the week, I schedule two or three poultry meals (we love chicken), one fish (we have a limited fondness for fish), two or three red meat (I buy lean), and an occasional meatless meal. To my meat or meatless base I add instant rice, noodles, or one of the pastas, plus a few vegetables selected to combine well and make a flavorful dish. As a binder most recipes suggest canned soup, but I prefer chicken or beef bouillon thickened with a white sauce or cornstarch. Herbs and spices add the final spark. All these main dishes need to complete the meal is a salad of some kind, a roll, and a beverage.

For a change of pace I resort to such quickies as fish fillets, ham steaks, beef steaks, hot dogs, hamburgers, or chicken pieces—cooked on the grill in summer—with microwaved potatoes, a cooked frozen or canned vegetable, and either a lettuce or cabbage salad. If I'm severely pressed for time, I serve the fresh greens in chunks instead of making a salad. Sliced fresh tomatoes and cucumbers offer welcome summer substitutes for salads and don't take much time.

Since our family has access to farm markets, I buy fresh sweet corn, fruit, and melons when available. Because I like menu variety and cold summer meals, I often switch our basic entrees in hot weather to salads made with a chicken, ham, hard-boiled egg and cheese, or seafood base.

I don't use recipes that call for exotic ingredients, and I try to keep on hand what I need to fill the recipes in my files. Peter and I usually decide on Saturday what we will eat the following week. I keep a list in my kitchen of supplies that are running low. When planning the next week's meals, I add to this list what we will need.

Sometimes Peter and I will change the meal plans while we are shopping. If fresh strawberries are in at the super-market or the fresh mushrooms look particularly good, or if we get a yen for something we haven't had in a long time or spot a tantalizing supermarket special, we depart from our plan. For the most part, though, we stick to it and find that it works—rarely do I have to throw anything out.

A friend of mine uses another type of quick-and-easy menu plan. She serves the same type of food each day of the week: a meat roast on Sunday, hamburgers every Monday, tuna or other fish casserole on Tuesdays, broiled chicken on Wednes-day, et cetera. Her menu plan lacks excitement—everybody in the family knows what is going to be on the table that night—but it gets the job done, and she feeds her family well.

One woman claims she cut her meal preparation time to ten minutes while still preserving a healthy diet. Her menus concentrate on fresh fruits and vegetables and grain prod-ucts. She uses very small portions of meats (especially the red meats) and no sauces or processed foods. Her typical menu is fruit or juice plus cereal or muffins for breakfast, sandwiches with fresh fruits or vegetable sticks for lunch, and soup and a salad or vegetables with rice for supper. Not a menu for everyone, but it works for her family and would for many.

Another family I know is fond of Italian foods. They cook pasta meals almost all of the time. This not only saves planning time, but it also limits the ingredients they need to keep on hand.

Beverly Mills and Alicia Ross in their syndicated column "Desperation Dinners" have come up with gourmet-style quickie meals that "taste good and are reasonably good for you." They doctor up quality convenience foods and take advantage of such shortcuts as pre-shredded cheese, pre-washed spinach, and bottled minced garlic.

Preparation Tips

You can get a head start on the week by cooking large quantities on the weekend for leftovers to be served later. I once found nine different ways to serve ham. I have a husband who cooks wonderful soups by the kettleful. They taste even better the next day, he says. Occasionally I make up a big batch of bran muffin mix that will keep for six weeks, and bake breakfast to order. You can also prepare extra portions of such items as pasta, rice, or cut-up veggies anytime to have on hand for nights later in the week when you are rushed or tired.

Other quick-preparation tips include:

• Keep your freezer stocked with meats, fish, and poultry packaged in one-meal portions. To defrost, pull out and refrigerate them the night before you will be serving them.

• Keep in frozen storage vegetables and vegetable blends, rolls, tortillas, and the like.

• Buy ahead and freeze your bread. To assure freshness, pull out and store in your breadbox only as much as you will be using within a few days.

• Work in pairs. Have another family member make the salad while you do the main dish.

• Do two things at once. While waiting for the fish to broil, start the vegetable or potatoes.

Finally, instead of always serving pizza on your ultra-busy or overly tired days, keep on hand continuously a ready supply of instant meals such as frozen dinners or packaged one-dish meals for last-minute emergencies.

Shopping Suggestions

Grocery-shopping time can be easily frittered away, so time-manage your shopping. Before you shop, plan for the week ahead so you will have what you need on hand, ready to cook, and won't need to stop at the store. If you plan carefully, you can get by with once-a-week trips except in summer when fresh fruits and produce are available. Even then, careful buying can minimize the need for more than one extra stop.

If you have a computer, you may want to computerize a list of the items you keep in your cupboards and refrigerator. As you run out of something, check it off the next week's list. Add to this the items you will need from the weekly menu plan you have drawn up, and your shopping list is complete. Sticking to the list will save you not only time but also money. For greater convenience, one woman has her list made out in order of the route she takes in her local supermarket.

Some women cut shopping time and money by buying in bulk. Again, keep a master list so you won't buy things you do not need. Paper products, cleaning supplies, pet food, toiletries, and baking supplies can all be purchased in quantity. Make sure you have sufficient storage space, and watch prices. You don't always save, and the time gained may not make buying in bulk worth it.

Save time by combining your grocery shopping with other errands and by shopping for everything at one time. Save even more time by doing all your shopping in one place. If your community does not have a mall that combines a supermarket with hardware, dry cleaning, and photo developing services, look for a shopping center where there is a grocery store en route.

If gardening is your hobby, include in your plantings, if possible, the food items you would otherwise be buying fresh midweek from a store.

Chart Your Mealtime Chores

Many families, especially large ones, post a kitchen chart for mealtime duties and change job assignments weekly. This prevents arguments among the children as to who is to do what, when. If a child will not be home to empty the dishwasher one night during the assigned week, make it her or his responsibility to exchange chores with a sibling who can.

It is more enjoyable for the family if members can have

their choice of duties. Almost everyone has jobs he or she dislikes. My husband hates washing dishes but doesn't mind drying. I don't mind either one, so I never ask him to wash. Younger children need to work all jobs until they learn them, but after that, volunteering for preferred tasks can be an option for them also.

Unfortunately, letting children select their chores does not always work. Sometimes everybody wants to sweep the floor or set the table, and nobody wants to load or unload the dishwasher. Your older teenage daughter may have to work over the supper hour, leaving her chores for the rest. If your family cannot work out a volunteer arrangement, try scheduling the duties for a time. Sometimes, when family members see that they cannot always have their favorite duty anyway, they are more open to taking less-preferred chores over those they detest.

To simplify food serving and reduce cleanup time, buy and use combination cooking/storage dishes. There are several kinds today, such as microwaveable serving bowls, glass baking dishes, and decorated saucepans. Buy dishes and utensils that look nice enough to put on the table. Try to match them to your dinnerware, and use them for serving. Make sure your selection is easy to clean, however, and immediately purchase the proper cleaning materials to keep them looking good.

Time-off-from-cooking Ideas

In most families Mom is in charge of the stove, but some of the world's best chefs are men. If you are married, why not make it a practice to have your husband cook one night a week, to give you a break? If he approves, let him conjure up his favorite meals. Cooking our favorite fare makes it more fun. In the summer, let him take charge of the grill.

You can also turn over the spatula occasionally to one or more of your teenagers. I taught all of my children how to cook, including our son. In today's world, knowing how to cook at least a few basic meals is a must. We once ended up with "barbaghetti" when Sue, who always cooked from memory, crossed in her mind the recipes for barbecue and spaghetti. Great family stories are made of such harmless foibles.

To ease the constant grind and enjoy a delightful time-off-from-cooking treat for everyone, why not plan to eat out regularly? When do your favorite restaurants have their weekday specials? Most food services cater to their slow business nights. Can your family work this night into your weekly schedule? If not, Friday is good because it sets a more relaxed pace for the weekend.

A friend of mine took turns with another friend entertaining each other's families for dinner every other week. Be creative. Could something like this work for you?

A much enjoyed time-off-from-cooking in our family was Sunday night fix-your-own. Not only could the children prepare whatever they wanted, but they could also violate my healthful eating standards. Some preposterous dishes, such as plain spaghetti without any butter or sauce, showed up. Crazy combinations of flour and who-knows-what went into the oven. We went through a lot of peanut butter. Once Sue wouldn't even eat what she made! But it was good fun. And blessed relief for Mom.

17

Practice Easy-living Home and Yard Care

On Judgment Day
If God should say
Did you clean your house today?
I will say, I did not.
I played with my children
And I forgot.

—Sue Wall

A 1991 survey of sixty thousand employees found that married women with full-time jobs still spend twice as many hours each week on household tasks as do their husbands. A dual-career couple may be able to maintain a balance of duties until the children arrive, but then the wife is usually left with an unequally large share. Single women, of course, have it the hardest. They have to handle all the duties themselves.

The bane of living for most modern women is housework. It wouldn't be so bad if we could do the job once and things would stay that way. The problem is, no matter how good a job we do, it has to be done all over again a short while later. One of my favorite books is Don Aslett's *Is There Life After Housework?* I say, "Yes! Absolutely! Whatever it takes to make the job simpler, quicker, and easier, let's go for it!"

Prevention Is the Best Answer

The best way to reduce housework is to prevent it in the first place. Experts agree that the most effective way to do that is to get rid of the excess clutter in your home. The less you have around, the less you have to repair, clean, *and* clean around.

Here are some guidelines to reducing clutter:

If you haven't used it in two years, get rid of it. You can give it to a friend or relative, have a rummage sale, put it in a consignment shop, give it to Goodwill, or trash it. The important thing is to dispose of it in one way or another. Reduce clutter in your clothes closets, linen closet, kitchen and bathroom cupboards, hardware drawer, the tool chest, and every drawer, cupboard, and storage space in your house. Don't forget all those assorted jackets in the front hall closet.

If you are married, have your husband go through his things and do the same. Help your children unclutter their rooms, especially the toy chest. Do the same in the attic, garage, laundry room, basement, and the rented storage unit—which you may find you no longer need!

A year after your first uncluttering free-for-all, do it again. At first, it is hard to let things go. Each time it gets easier.

If you are a dyed-in-the-wool saver, try boxing up your excess goods and dating the box. Don't label what is in it except for "clothes," "kitchen stuff," and the like. If you haven't missed any of the items two or three years later, get rid of the box without looking inside. If you do remove something, keep that and dump the rest after three years.

If you have two or more items that do the same job, dispose of all but one. Do you have two food processors, one large and one mini? Do you really need both? Do you have two metal polishes? furniture polishes? window cleaners? floor waxes? oven cleaners? Use up the extra one and don't replace it.

How many fountain pens do you really need? How many back issues of your favorite magazines? How many storage boxes of different sizes do you need for gift-giving? Set a limit for each and stick to it.

Give away outdated items. Is that extra pair of glasses no longer in your prescription range? Is that skirt out of style? Are you storing tires for a vehicle you no longer own? What more need I say?

Put an end to your unfinished projects. How long has it been since you worked on it? If it has been three years or more, discard it.

Unclutter Your Lifestyle

Place items close to where they will be used. Put the key rack near the door into the garage. Store pots and pans next to the stove, silverware and dishes near the kitchen table or dishwasher—preferably between them.

Store seldom-used items in out-of-the-way places. Items such as flower vases, "company" serving dishes, and the waffle iron should be relegated to higher shelves and far corners.

Handle things once. Don't have temporary holding areas. When you take your jacket off, put it directly into the closet. When the mail comes in, place it immediately on the desk where you pay the bills. Unload your groceries where they will be stored (refrigerator, pantry, or cupboard). If a bag contains mixed items, reload those needing refrigeration into the sack with the cold-storage items. When all bags are unpacked, carry that bag over to the refrigerator and unload it.

Store your important papers in one storage unit. Keep your tax forms, receipts, warranties, vital family correspondence, and the like together in a file cabinet or cardboard storage box. Valuables should be stored together in a bank deposit box or an insulated home safe.

Discard sentimental deadwood. Are you keeping an item just because someone you care about once gave it to you? Do you still want it? If it has lost its meaningfulness, usefulness, or value, get rid of it. Screen your home for these kinds of articles and dispose of them.

Other Prevention Tips

Prevent damage by using corner protectors for wall corners that are apt to get chipped or dirtied by passing traffic.

Buy artificial plants, to keep things tidy. Or, if you are an avid plant lover like me, cluster your live ones and display them together. They like the company, and it is easier to water them. A pebble tray under your grouping will help prevent water damage to the floor or carpet, and if kept wet, will provide the humidity most plants like.

Choose pets wisely. Does your family just "have to have" a dog? Pick a little one (smaller messes to clean up) with short hair (no need to groom and less need to brush frequently), and train the dog well. A well-trained dog will do less overall damage to your home and yard and minimize the need to hunt for a lost beloved pet.

Child-proof your decor. Install carpets and floorings that don't show lint, and use large mats inside the exterior doors to collect tracked-in dirt. Some mats work better than others; find ones that do a good job. Natural wood paneling and woodwork don't show handprints nearly as much as painted ones. Washable wallpapers are easy to maintain. Put protective grills over the screening in the storm doors.

Keep dirt outside. Some families have their children leave their shoes at the door. (They already leave their winter boots there, I hope!) This doesn't always work; sometimes children just track in the dirt on their socks or bare feet. If you follow this practice, have a box for shoes by the doorway, and keep socks or slippers there for family members to wear around the house.

Put child-height clothes hooks in the closet adjacent to the door the children use most. Make sure your exterior doors have springs that close without much effort on the child's part. Designate their toys as "indoor" and "outdoor," restrict use accordingly, and store the outdoor ones in the garage.

Install an air conditioner, if possible. Not only does it allow you to keep the windows closed against windstorms and excess humidity in the summer, but it also filters and cleans the air, providing more comfort for family members who have allergies.

Eliminate food mess. When and if family members want to snack in rooms other than the kitchen (and if you permit it), have them carry their snacks on food trays. Make it a rule that each returns his or her tray to the kitchen after each use.

Get Help

If you can afford it, hire someone to do your housekeeping. It is an indulgence that frees up time for precious family and personal concerns. A cleaning service may not be as expensive as you think. My daughters find that having their house cleaned every other week is sufficient.

Can't afford to hire someone to do it? Spread the work around. Your children, including the boys, need to learn how to care for possessions. Many young men, and some older ones, are living alone today. Even though it may not bother them as much as it does women, they really don't like to live in dust and clutter, and a clean home is also more healthful.

In our family the children always cleaned their own rooms. If it didn't get done, they had to live in their own messes. I didn't admonish them. If it bothered me at times, I just closed their doors. If and when they couldn't find things, they knew exactly who was at fault, so they couldn't complain. Oddly, they all went through periods of neatness and periods of messiness, as though they had to try out both. I think it worked well. They all keep a comfortable balance in their own homes today. (Homes can be so neat that they are unlivable.)

Make it a rule in your house that the persons who do a task may do it their way. This eases stress on everyone. If your son wants the garbage dumped and sealed in plastic bags to carry it out to the trash, family members should accommodate him. If your daughter wants to dust the furniture with a feather duster instead of a cloth and polish, why not let her? People differ in their preferences, and these preferences should be respected. I like to use a sponge for wiping kitchen counters; all of my daughters prefer using dishcloths. To each her own. The object is to get the job done satisfactorily and in good time. As long as these objectives are met, what does it matter how the person goes about it?

Again, give family members a choice of housekeeping tasks, whenever possible. One young couple shares house-cleaning duties on a 70-30 percent basis, with the wife taking the larger share, and reverses the percentages when it comes to yard care.

Simplified Housekeeping Guidelines

Doris Janzen Longacre in *Living More With Less* quotes a neighbor who moved to Pennsylvania from England: "The first few months I went out every day and washed or swept the front steps. Then one day I looked up and down the street and realized that nobody else bothered much with what in England is a real mark of a good housekeeper. So I quit cleaning my steps! But what is it that one has to do here?"

Every community and culture has unspoken standards, Longacre says. In Indonesia it is sweeping the packed earth around your house at least once, if not twice, a day. Years ago in North America, it was who got the sheets out on the line first on Monday morning, and how white they were.

Get out of the "minimum standards" mentality. We need not follow cultural expectations. When cleaning, use the simplest and easiest techniques you can find. I once ran across a timely, very practical bathroom cleaning guide: clean it as you use it. After finishing your shower, wipe down the walls. Are you brushing your teeth into a grimy sink? Store a sponge and cleanser in a handy spot and wipe it out then and there. Keep a brush in a container right next to the toilet and train your family members to use it whenever they soil the bowl.

Clean as you go, everywhere. In the kitchen, whenever you use a pan just to heat water, dry it and put it away. Keep a hand dishwasher (refillable bottle with screw-top brush) on the sink to use whenever you have just one or two dishes to clean, and take care of these tiny jobs immediately.

Make the bed as you get out of it. My husband gets up fifteen minutes ahead of me, so I do my side when I arise and one of us does his later. Or skip making the bed occasionally and keep the door closed. Who cares?

As for weekly cleaning, Jeff Campbell has laid out in his book *Speed Cleaning* a quick, efficient method for cleaning a house in minimum time. He tells what tools and products work most effectively and explains how to work your way through the house without doing unnecessary work or back-tracking. He claims a home can be cleaned so thoroughly in little more than an hour that it may need only semi-weekly or monthly attention. Many of his ideas work well; however, his book does not cover everyday picking up or heavy-duty cleaning chores (oven and spring cleaning).

Use the proper tools. I smeared my windows for years whenever I washed them, despite going over them several times. In reading Don Aslett's book I discovered the magic of the squeegee. Once I started using one, I washed and squeegeed one time only in one-fourth my customary time and no longer got smears. Also, use cleansing agents properly; they are chemicals. They work by creating a reaction. To minimize scrubbing time and effort, give them time to work.

Do the Hard Part First

When planning a family day that includes housecleaning, start with the heavy-duty part—the housecleaning. You'll all tend to get it done faster so you can get to the fun part.

For radicals like me who truly hate housework and will do anything to get out of it, don't schedule your housecleaning. Clean only when and where the dust and dirt bothers you. Wash only those windows that frame a desired view and cover the rest with sheer curtains or blinds. Power clean only when your husband starts writing on the furniture, company is coming, or the grime is really getting to you.

Once a year, have a blitzkrieg. Spring cleaning is not quite so disheartening as the endless weekly cleaning chore. The spirit really moves me when the windows can fly open and fresh warm breezes flutter in. Repair, unclutter, wash windows, shampoo the carpets, wax the vinyl floors, touch up furniture nicks, and just generally fix and freshen the house. It feels good, salves the guilties, and picks up what gets left undone the rest of the year.

Avoid Washday Blues

To cut laundering time, treat stains with a stain stick as you undress. Stains remove more easily when they are promptly treated, and you are less apt to forget or overlook the stain. Have your family do the same. Stop buying clothes that need dry cleaning or ironing (insofar as you can). And don't change the sheets every week. Change them when they need it.

Have the older children do their own laundry. They are much less apt to change clothes two or three times a day when they see how much extra work it makes.

Easy Home Maintenance

The best thing you can do to get maximum use and minimum repair on any home appliance is to read and follow the manufacturer's instructions for operation and cleaning. It sounds so simple, but many people do not take the time. Doing so may prevent unnecessary breakdowns and repair bills, and your appliances will last longer.

Discard small appliances when they break down. If it's a problem you can fix easily, such as replacing an electrical cord plug, set the item aside and note immediately on the family calendar when you will fix it. If you can't find time on the calendar, throw it out. You haven't the time.

When doing occasional house repair and lawn care jobs, consider renting the equipment. You don't really need to have a fertilizer spreader or leaf blower around all the time. And they have to be stored somewhere—usually in the way. Save your money for such vital purchases as the lawnmower and, in north country, the snowblower.

When you buy items for your home, keep them simple. The more they do, the faster and easier they break down. Two friends of mine had their energy-efficient furnaces go out on them in severe winter weather. In one case, the water pipes froze and shattered, causing considerable damage. My husband and I were advised by a professional serviceman to retain our older model until it wore out, just to prevent such a problem.

Simple Yard Care

For easy yard care, use a thick mulch or decorative stone under the landscape plantings around your house. This avoids the need for weeding. Cluster decorative plantings into a few selected areas that provide a nice view or accent the house. The plants should be far enough apart so they will not crowd one another and need to be separated or removed when they are full grown. Keep the plan simple; a minimal planting can be as lovely if not more so than an elaborate one. It all depends on the setting and the types of plants used.

If your lawn is bluegrass, fertilize it "when the growing's good"—early fall and early spring. Lay off in the summer when the weeds grow best and the lawn goes dormant. Water the lawn deeply and not too often, and let the grass grow two inches high or taller. It keeps the lawn healthier.

If your lawn is larger than you want to care for and your zoning and neighbors will permit it, plant a small wilderness area of prairie grasses or turn part of your lawn over to ground cover. My in-laws had no lawn at all. Living in woods, they simply lined the path to the house in myrtle, and it was lovely.

Limit your flower beds to what you can handle easily—a few flower boxes, a couple of container planters around the patio, or perhaps some hanging planters. If you have to have a flower border, keep it small and mulch between the perennial or annual plants until they fill the space. One gardener I knew minimized weeding by designing her garden so that the plants would grow together and choke out the weeds. This method takes time to develop, but it works.

18

Exercise Good Car Care

"Everything in life is somewhere else, and you get there in a car."

—E. B. White

Cars are indispensable in today's society. We can't live without them, and we can't forgive them when they break down on us. They rob us of time, energy, money, and peace of mind.

The easy-living antidote to this is to follow a few practices that minimize the chances you will run into trouble. The golden rule of low-stress car ownership is to buy right, take good care, and repair or replace at the proper time.

Buy Right

Unless you were born with a wrench in your back pocket, the best way to have a serviceable, dependable vehicle is to buy a late-model car and keep it until it gets to the problem-running stage. New cars generally hold up well, but sometimes they have bugs that need to be worked out. New car buyers also strike out occasionally. Although many states have "lemon laws," one still has to contend with the stress and inconvenience of dealing with problems.

You can generally get the service history on a late-model car these days. Good ones usually stay in the area. If your prospective buy has been picked up at a car auction, be suspicious. It most likely has had heavy mileage or has been in a major accident—both suggesting major trouble ahead.

Ask your dealer for the history, and call the previous owner to confirm the facts. You could have an excellent buy. Many people who have new car mania trade in sound vehicles in excellent condition after a few years. Let someone else break it in, and you cash in on the best years. Make that "second best years" if newness and/or status are important to you.

Before purchasing a used car, have an independent repairman look it over. A good mechanic will know what to look for to confirm the mileage and condition. Has the oil pan gasket been replaced? If so, there has probably been major engine trouble. Are the brake and accelerator pads too worn or not worn enough (already replaced)? These are good indicators of age. Are the axles straight? They are when they leave the factory, but that can change after a bad collision.

Sometimes car manufacturers offer full maintenance and repair service with the sales of their vehicles, both old and new. One of my daughters had trouble with hers while on a trip hundreds of miles from home. A dealer in another state did some repair work that she later learned didn't need to be done. Her local dealer helped her get her money back, amounting to hundreds of dollars. You can't beat that!

Take Good Care

Read and follow your car manual. The manufacturer knows best how to keep its vehicles running effectively. This one practice alone will do more to help you keep your automobile on the road and running well than anything else.

That said, here are the guidelines to proper maintenance:

1. *Get the oil changed every 2500-3000 miles.* Clean oil running through the cylinders keeps the engine-burning process cleaner, prolonging the life of the engine and all its parts.

When you have the work done, get a "full service" oil

change—one that includes a "lube job." With full service the mechanic checks the car's transmission, power steering, windshield wash, and battery fluids. He greases all of the fittings and checks such important operating items as the differential, air filter, windshield wipers, and tire pressure.

2. *Watch your tires.* Do they look a little flat? Inflate them to the correct tire pressure. If you don't know what that is, consult your service garage or lube service. If your tire is completely flat, change it on the spot or have a service person do so. Driving on it wrecks not only the tire but also the rim. Rotate the tires periodically.

Buy new tires when the tread depth is getting low. You cannot ride safely on worn tires. You are risking skids on wet or snowy pavements and reducing your chances of a quick stop in the event of an accident. Worn tires can also blow out and cause an accident.

3. *Tune the engine.* The timetable for tune-ups on cars varies, so check your manufacturer's instructions as to how often your car needs one done. Some newer cars do not need them often. Tuning the engine times the firing of the spark plugs so that the pistons operate at peak efficiency and with a minimum of gas consumption.

4. *Wash off road grit and grime frequently and wax the car* occasionally to keep up your car's finely-polished finish.

If you are going on a long trip—more than 1000 miles— check before you go to see if you are due for an oil change or tuneup. If your car is of an older vintage, you may want your service garage to check for signs of wear or pending break-down before you leave.

When It's Time to Repair

If your car is working well, don't worry about it except to change the oil frequently and keep an eye on the tires. Simple, isn't it? Many old cars need little more than this— perhaps replacement of the windshield wipers, a paint touchup or paint job, and timely exhaust system replacement.

Your car can't last forever, however. Just as people get sick, cars act up now and then. If and when your car is not operating the way it should, get it repaired promptly. If you hear rattles or other engine noises that were not there before, have them checked out. If the engine is running roughly, if it seems to bounce instead of hum, it is telling you it needs work done to it. If your car suddenly sounds like a fire truck, its exhaust system probably needs to be replaced.

Most of all, if you see steam rise from beneath the hood, stop wherever you are and *do not drive* the car any farther. Call for service or have it towed. If you keep on going, the car will soon run dry and freeze up the engine. If this happens, the engine must be replaced—a monumental bill—or you will need to purchase another vehicle. Yet very often, when steam rises, all that is needed is to replace a few inexpensive water hoses.

The other great danger to your car is to have it run out of oil. That also freezes up the engine. Watch for oil leaks on your garage floor or driveway. If the car is burning oil, monitor the oil level closely until the engine is replaced or you trade in your vehicle.

Your best friend when it comes to keeping a car running is a good service garage. Find one where the workmanship is reliable (ask people for their recommendations), and build a friendly relationship with the mechanics there. Not only can good repairpersons assist you in selecting a reliable buy in a car, but they will also advise you on how to care for it if you ask questions when you bring it in for servicing. Some will even give you a loaner vehicle while your car is laid up, although this practice is becoming less prevalent.

Have a backup plan ready for when your car is out of service. If you are a dual-career family, you may be able to share the use of your husband's car. But what if he is out of town or needs his car that day? Do you have business associates living in your area who could pick you up? Could you use an inexpensive rental car for a day or two? Find out in advance what your community has available. Cars that are out of service are a normal fact of life. It is less stressful if you have at least two or three options when it happens to you.

There comes a time with cars when little problems start

cropping up here and there every time you turn around. This means a lot of stress and frustration lie ahead. When your car starts needing repairs frequently, replace it as soon as you are able. This is the time to let teenage or adult amateur mechanics who love to tinker with cars and engines have a go at it. Its best, most useful life is gone. Say goodbye to it, sell it, and buy another.

19

Plan Restful Leisure and Family Celebrations

Is rest important? Surely so. "God blessed the seventh day and hallowed it, because on it God rested from all the work that he had done in creation" (Genesis 2:3). "After [Jesus] had dismissed the crowds, he went up the mountain by himself to pray" (Matthew 14:23).

The Lord himself took time to rest after completing the creation. Christ left thronging crowds on several occasions to go up into the hills to pray, probably leaving behind many people who could have used his help. If our perfect God felt rest was essential, how much more ought we.

Restful leisure, low-stress vacations, and meaningful holidays and celebrations round out a balanced easy-living lifestyle. But too often "restful" is the farthest thing from reality. Your after-work schedule is a race to get your teenage son to his part-time job and the other kids to their soccer games, 4-H meetings, or church choir rehearsals. Or perhaps you, or you and your husband, are taking classes essential to improving your job skills or opportunities for advancement. For your family, dinner is a when-you-can-grab-a-bite proposition. You fall into bed later than you would like, without having had a meaningful conversation with anyone in the family all evening.

An occasional day like the above can be justified, but if this frantic pace is par for the course in your house, it's time for reassessment. Rest is important to your good health. A relaxed or semi-relaxed atmosphere in your household and some good solid communication may be more important than many of the things you or your family members are involved in. Your children get only one chance to grow up. Do you want their idea of family life to be a constant merry-go-round? Do you want *yours* to be?

For Leisurely Weeknights . . .

We've already mentioned in this book many ways by which you could downsize the demands made on family members. The hardest part is sitting down together and deciding on what changes each family member will make to enable an easier pace. Talk with your family to see how they feel about *their* daily pace. If you or they feel a downshift is in order, give them a few days to think about what they are willing to give up. Then meet again to revise the family schedule and put a new one in place.

For fun in the summer, plan special treats with your family—a quick trip to the lake after work or a drive to the Dairy Queen after supper. Does your community have summer theatre? Would your family enjoy taking in community or church league ball games? If nothing else, how about a dip in the local community swimming pool on a too-hot night?

Can you negotiate with your boss to start work earlier so you have more evening time with your summer vacationers? Can you drop part of your workload for a few months to free up some time? Could you sneak in a long weekend—Friday through Monday—sometime during the summer? If you do your own housework, could you hire a commercial service just for the summer, to give you extra time with the family at this delightful time of the year?

For Restful Weekends . . .

Weekends are often a maze of scattered activity for today's families. Are yours? If so, what a waste of precious time!

Weekends constitute more than one third of our lives, all of it relatively free time for most of us. A little attention and planning can turn this valuable commodity into a more meaningful experience for you and your family.

First, try to avoid bringing home work from the office over the weekend. It would be better to spend additional time at the office during the week, if necessary. Try to do some chores during the week. Can the laundry be done on one or more weekday nights? Can you and the family clean one room a night on a weekday? Or can you schedule a one-night blitz where everyone pitches in to help clean the main living areas—the kitchen, bath, and living and family rooms?

Can you find no time during the week? Then try working together on the weekends. Some families organize and share their Saturday chores to open up some free time together. One family does it this way: each member cleans his or her own room and one other room early on Saturday morning, completes an assigned portion of yardwork, and then at the supermarket fills a list given him or her by the parent. "We zoom in and out of the market in twenty minutes," says this mother, "so we can have more time to play."

Plan your fun times, and include the whole family in the planning. That way everyone agrees with and anticipates upcoming events. Don't assume you know your children's wishes. Children, like all of us, have minds of their own and change them frequently.

Be prepared to shift gears. A family member can become sick. Or weather can change plans. An occasional spontaneous activity is a refreshing and blessed relief from a regimented existence. And all of us benefit from having nothing to do every so often.

Once in a while, do something special on your family weekend time together. Explore a new museum or trek to a park or nearby tourist attraction you have never visited before. What part of your community have you never taken time to see? Twenty years after moving into the area, my husband and I finally took time to visit a historic home here. I was entranced by the elegant way of life my community forebears established in a state sparsely settled at the time.

Look for opportunities to engage in some one-on-one time with each child. Weekends usually offer the best chance for bonding. This is especially important if your child is a teenager and communication is in short supply.

Don't expect your teenagers to participate in every family activity. This is their time of life to move away from their dependence on the family. One of their ways to break too-tight bonds is to do things with friends or just to say no to family events now and then.

It's Vacation Time

One of the musts for New Jersey's Governor Christine Todd Whitman in raising her children was "to go away together for a vacation where we are just a family."

Vacations, like weekends, are best planned together during your "family time." The watchword is *easy does it*. Don't plan to go too far, and don't schedule too much to do. Vacation time should be a time to relax, not run the frantic pace you get caught up in at home, or one that is worse.

Vacations at home can be great if you do things that differ from what you do on your usual weekend. Most people travel long distances to see tourist meccas, neglecting those near home. As an alternative, why not try visits to nearby treasures, both for the relaxation of not having to travel far and for the cost savings.

When going on a trip, pack light and smart. Plan your clothing needs around one basic color so you only need one extra pair of shoes. Coordinate a couple of blouses or shirts around each pair of pants or skirt. Have your teens do the same. If they object, have them carry their own luggage and/or pay the extra airline cost for an overweight bag. Nothing works better and with less pain than using real-life consequences to get teens to change their minds.

Be prepared for emergencies. Bring along an extra pair of

eyeglasses, and refill medicine prescriptions before leaving. Have a way to keep track of your children so they don't get lost in crowds. Many large families pack and dress their brood in the same color T-shirts—a bright, easily spotted hue—for quick, easy identification. And be sure to tell the children what to do if they get lost.

Take precautions against thievery. Thieves prey on tourists because tourists generally carry a lot of money, and a small crime isn't worth prosecuting in a community far from home. Carry your money in safe ways, and avoid high-risk areas.

Something always goes wrong on a vacation, even with the best-laid plans. Some tourist attractions you expected to see will be closed, or a planned route will be detoured. Plan extra time into your schedule for delays or detours. Plan a little more in case you discover unexpected treasures along the way that you want to take in. If you don't need the additional time, you will just get home a little earlier and have more time to relax before getting back into your regular schedule— a bonus!

Finally, allow plenty of time the day before you leave to make last-minute preparations, and plan to return in sufficient time to wind down before returning to school and work. A bad send-off or a frazzled return can take the pleasurable edge off the most memorable vacation trip.

Plan an occasional vacation getaway just for you and your spouse, especially when the children are older. Teenage kids love it! They look forward to being on their own. When we made these ventures, we always had a neighbor on call for advice or emergencies, but the children never needed it.

Enjoy Some Solitude

Once in awhile, retreat. Take a day, or a week, or a couple of weeks off from the constant grind of demands, pressures, deadlines, phone calls, traffic, noise, and people needing you, and spend this time in solitude. Sit quietly on a park bench. Hike a favorite trail. Or browse the stacks at your local library. Some churches plan weekend women's retreats for their members. If this appeals to you, go.

Solitude relieves tension. It puts us back in touch with our priorities and goals. It lets us explore our inner, deeper needs. It brings us closer to God. It uncovers the simple pleasures life offers.

To experience solitude, you don't need to get away from people entirely. What you do need is to get away from those people and activities that make demands on you. My husband and I like to retreat together, camping in the off-season or in parks that are apt to be nearly empty. We read and loaf, sharing minimal cooking and other essential tasks.

Don't use this time to saunter through the mall; you might find the very sweater your daughter has been looking for and put yourself back on the demands track again.

If you are planning to retreat alone and have not done so before, explain to your family what you are doing and why, so they won't worry. Solitude is a rare, unrecognized value in our culture. Few people understand or appreciate it in our present-day world. Fortunately, that is changing.

Spend Some God-Time Together

The sabbath was instituted by the Lord not just as a day of rest, but also to allow us to step back from life and survey what we are doing and where we are going. It gives us an opportunity to appreciate God and what he has done, just as God himself did after the creation. "God saw everything that he had made, and indeed, it was very good" (Genesis 1:31).

A faith life is not only a basic personal need, but it is also an important part of everyday family living. Foster good spiritual habits in your children by worshiping together on Sunday and participating as a family in church programs. Many churches are starting to hold Family Nights.

For many families whose roots and childhood families are elsewhere, church is becoming "family." Former bishop Herbert Chilstrom of the Evangelical Lutheran Church in America claims the church best serves the need for "family." Pointing out that many people today (singles, widows or widowers, divorced, adopted persons, gays and lesbians, prison inmates, and the elderly in nursing homes), have no family in the traditional sense of the word, he quotes the words of Jesus: "Whoever does the will of my Father in heaven is my brother and sister and mother" (Matthew 12:50). Blood may be thicker than water, he says, but "faith is thicker than blood." Many persons have found their true "home" in belonging to a caring church.

Some families may have the opportunity to schedule as their vacation Family Week at their area church camp. This combines family and faith. Our family had two such experiences in different camps in separate states, and we enjoyed them both. Each camp is only as good as the program is enjoyable. A given program may not be to your liking. So that you will know what to expect, check with persons who have attended in the past. Memories of successful family camping events are priceless.

Family Traditions and Celebrations

Traditions, holidays, and family celebrations of key events in the lives of family members cement family ties. Dining together is one of the strongest traditions. Sharing food has a way of breaking down barriers and encouraging people to draw closer. According to one study, as we entered the nineties more than half of American families were still eating dinner together almost every night. Low- to middle-income families are more apt to dine together than upper-income families. The higher the income, the less likely it is that families do so.

Ninety-seven percent of Americans spend one or more holidays each year with their families. Christmas and Thanksgiving top the list, but such holidays as Easter, Independence Day, Labor Day, and even Valentine's Day are often celebrated by families. Eighty-three percent of the population begins holiday meals with a prayer or grace, and almost half begin every meal the same way. Families travel thousands of miles to attend a relative's wedding and renew old family ties. Baptisms, confirmations, graduations, and funerals give rise to elaborate family gatherings. Sharing these moments provides the opportunity to confirm our common faith and support one another at critical points in a family member's life. Key times, both happy and unhappy, are high-stress times. Joy is sweeter and sorrow diminished when we share the load with one or more persons who care. Family celebrations do just that.

Christmas is meant for worship and for sharing God's extraordinary love, as revealed in Jesus' birth, with your family. If your holiday is frazzled, that truth gets smothered. If that is what is happening to you, rethink your Christmas. How can you get it to where you want it to be?

Plan for the holiday well ahead of time, so that you can coast through it smoothly. Take in only those events that are important to you and/or your family, and don't expect everything to be picture perfect, as the media portray. Take what comes and enjoy it.

At important family celebrations, avoid getting caught in the commercial trap. Dispense with gift giving if it is nothing more than an obligation. Follow your heart, not cultural expectations. Cards are good alternatives to gifts in some situations. Your presence is often the best gift you can give.

Sometimes the most appropriate response is to do nothing. The last Christmas gift we gave my aging father-in-law was the book *Old Friends*, the story of a supportive friendship between two residents of a nursing home. Unfortunately, his mental state had already deteriorated too much to appreciate it.

Weddings do not belong only to the bride and groom, nor funerals to the deceased, nor birthdays to the child. These celebrations have little meaning without the participation of the guests. Bear this in mind in your planning and participation. The bridal couple who say, "We can invite only those whom we choose," ignore the scale of the rite of passage. Parents are dealing with the loss of a child, happy though it may be. Their input recognizes the full scale of such an event. Family members who say, when making funeral arrangements, "Dad would have wanted this . . ." lack insight into the fact that the primary purpose of funerals is to help the bereaved deal with their loss. The needs of the bereaved should be foremost. With birthdays, parents need not feel the birthday child should have whatever he or she wants. This is a good occasion to teach the child that such celebrations are family affairs, not opportunities for personal indulgence.

If attending a family event is painful due to a stressful interfamily conflict, focus on the true value of your being there. By attending, will you be able to contribute anything to the family's well-being and solidarity? In some cases, the answer may be no. In others, where your questioning revolves around actions you do not approve, attending may be the best thing you can do. It is your way of saying you love these persons and recognize and accept their right to make their own decisions, even as you question their judgment. If in doubt, pray for wisdom and direction.

If your home and family obligations and circumstances necessitate that you say no to an important family celebration, don't feel guilty if family members are miffed. Of such things family feuds are made, but this is your decision, not theirs. They have no right to question your judgment. If you make your decision with the help of God, you can be at peace.

20

Control Your Money and Spending

*"Keep your lives free from the love of money, and
be content with what you have; for he has said, 'I
will never leave you or forsake you.'"*
—Hebrews 13:5

In their book *'Tis a Gift to Be Simple,* Barbara DeGrote-Sorenson and her husband David state: "In our family we have a game we play with our kids when wandering the halls of a store with enticing merchandise. Any parent knows the tirade of demands children can make when they are over-stimulated with so much stuff. The 'I want that!' demand in our family has been changed to 'I like that!' Our children are allowed to like as much as they want, and they are comfortable with the fact that they don't have to own it to like it. Most of the time [liking it] is enough for them."

Money and the things it buys can easily become the tyrannical master of our lives. Modern advertising methods and cultural expectations (You are entitled to *have it all!*) lead many well-intentioned people to spend to excess. Are you a slave to money, or is it your slave? You have a choice. If you want a low-stress life, you and your family have to be in control of your overall spending.

Controlled spending doesn't just reduce tension. It sets a pace of moderation and contentment that casts a rosy glow over the entire climate of your home. You do not have to live at the cliff's edge to find enjoyment and satisfaction. Living behind the driver's wheel on a pleasant sunny road is much more relaxing and gratifying.

If your family spending is not under control, detect where the trouble is coming from. There could be several causes. Is your family's appetite for material goods demanding more from the family income than it can handle? Or are you just not saving enough for emergencies? Is it that your income and savings are sufficient but you have no idea where all the money is going? Different sources of difficulty call for different solutions.

Downsize Your Demands

If rampant materialism is making life miserable for your family, downsizing family demands is your remedy. Financial strains and indebtedness are one of the greatest triggers of severe stress. Downsizing your family's demands not only makes life more affordable, but it will also make it more bearable if a job loss or other money crisis comes along.

We never know when that might happen. A number of years ago one of my daughters had the engine go out on her car just after the warranty had expired. (Doesn't it always happen that way?) Because it was a foreign car, no rebuilt engines were available, and the cost of a new engine ran into thousands of dollars. But the car was too young to junk and too disabled to resell, so she had no choice but to purchase a new engine.

To downsize your demands, decide as a family that you are going to change the status quo and do things differently. Determine to live light. Depending on their ages, all family members can help prioritize the family's discretionary spending until a comfortable level is reached.

Making the decision together as a family assures that

everyone will cooperate. No one wants to be the one to ruin a family effort. There is a second benefit to having the children join the discussion and decision making: You are simultaneously teaching them to respect the value of money and the importance of fiscal responsibility.

You may want to have your children budget their allowances as part of this process. This will help them learn that they cannot have everything they want without exceeding their income. They can see firsthand how placing a relative value on everything still allows them to purchase what they want most. And they can come to realize that not having everything really doesn't change their life or happiness very much.

Downsize in major ways by reducing your housing expense, grocery bill, transportation costs, clothing costs, and home furnishing expenses. Housing is the big-ticket item, but changing housing is an expensive proposition if you own your home. Whether or not to attack the cost of housing depends on the extent of your financial discomfort and your vulnerability to and likelihood of a job or other income loss.

Groceries run second and offer greater opportunities to save. Costs can be cut easily by purchasing fresh produce such as strawberries or sweet corn only when they are in season and reasonably priced and by avoiding high-cost shelf items. You can also save by planning your meals around the less-expensive meats and meatless menus. Try generic products. Some generics lack taste quality, but many are as delicious and nutritious as their equivalent expensive brands.

Transportation costs are somewhat negotiable. If you are a new-car addict or a sports-car buff, you already know where to cut and how much you can save. But if your present vehicles are modest, you haven't much maneuvering room. You need dependable transportation to get back and forth to work if public transportation is not convenient. You can compromise a bit by selecting lower-cost car models, but only on that point, as was pointed out in the chapter on car care.

Clothing and home furnishings expenses are discretionary. The big cost challenge with clothes is to avoid following fashion fads, and the biggest hurdle for most families is teen pressure to follow the crowd. At this vulnerable age, teens want to be accepted, to fit in with their peers. In modern society that has come to be identified with wearing certain clothing items. How your family handles this is up to you. Cutting out faddish purchases can be a welcome opportunity to help your teen form a more solid set of values. But if your teen is having serious adjustment difficulties, giving in on the clothing budget might be justified as "not sweating the small stuff" for the sake of helping a struggling loved one avert more serious problems.

Keep your home decor simple. Does your house resemble something out of a magazine, or does it reflect your family's tastes, values, and lifestyle? Homes are not showcases; they are places to live. As Doris Longacre says in *Living More With Less*, "Home has more to do with friends and love than with expansive family rooms." Be content with what you need in order to do the job you want done. And don't replace your home furnishings just because styles change; wait until they *need* replacement.

Save in Small Ways

You may be able to downsize your spending by rethinking your buying habits and the way you shop. Are you accustomed to buying on impulse things that look good to you in ads or when you pass by them in a store? Get in the habit of thinking about prospective purchases overnight. Do you still want the item the next day? Or was your impulse just a rush that fades in the light of serious consideration? Ask yourself, "Will I really use this? How often? Does that justify the cost and the need to store it?" This guideline alone has saved me hundreds, if not thousands of dollars.

Another way to curb unnecessary spending is to ask the right question. Instead of asking, "Do I need this?" ask yourself, "Can I get along comfortably without it?"

Save by easing up on gift giving. Give hand-crafted or homemade items, such as gourmet breads. Give your time instead of purchased gifts. I like to give my daughters the gift of babysitting engagements. They love it! Their biggest aggravation in life is getting and keeping dependable sitters.

Save in little ways by living thriftily. For example, I save dishwasher detergent by rinsing my dishes before stacking them in the dishwasher and using the first wash cycle as a prerinse (no detergent). One item here or there may not get clean, but that sometimes happens when I use both cycles as wash cycles. I just rewash in the machine or hand wash these items.

Recycle your plastic or paper grocery bags by using them as wastebasket liners. Save packing boxes to use as storage containers. Reuse bushel baskets or fruit carriers to collect yard and garden debris. Shop rummage and garage sales for items you might need.

Do away with unnecessary debt. Borrow only for the biggest-ticket items—your house and essential cars. Don't buy on time payments anything you don't have to have. Save the money and pay cash. Pay off your charge cards monthly, before interest accrues. Not only does this save interest money, but it also prevents the charge cards from building to unmanageable levels.

Save by making your own entertainment as a family—storytelling, reading to each other, group singing—or take in your community's free summer band concerts. Have the family pack their lunches instead of purchasing them. When you eat out, frequent lower-cost restaurants.

Many restaurants serve oversized portions. If you patronize one of these, why not ask if you can split your meal? Ask for the large-size beverage and an extra glass and split that too. Or ask for the senior citizen's meal. In some restaurants the child's meal will do the job, except for growing teens or those who work out-of-doors or at physically demanding jobs.

Not all of these ways to downsize are right for everyone. Because needs differ, you will need to decide what will work for you and your family. The important thing is to keep your focus on your goal—controlling your spending for more comfortable living.

Easy Money Management

If confusion over your managing your money is plaguing your serenity, look for the reason. Do you have an adequate emergency savings account? Though the need is not usually as great for dual income families as it is where there is a single breadwinner, many people today still short themselves this essential ingredient to low-stress living.

Experts suggest that you set aside an amount equal to three to six months' income. The amount depends on how solid your job and income situations are and what other sources of funds you have available. Are you subject to a strike or layoff? Then obviously you should have more. You can get along with less if you have 401K funds or family members who could loan you money. If your job is one in which your income fluctuates wildly, a full year's income is recommended.

If your management confusion stems from a proliferation of checking and investment accounts, look for an easier management system. The more accounts you have, the more confusing your bookkeeping and the more complex your tax reporting becomes. Try consolidating. Can you operate all household monies from one checkbook? If this is awkward for you and your husband, have one of you work out of the checkbook and the other carry enough cash to last until the next payday.

Limit your mutual funds to a few that do the job you want done. Most experts agree that as long as you pick a reputable family of funds, it does not matter much which one you invest with in the long run. If you want to diversify, do so within your fund family.

For ease and safety in money handling, dispense with all but one of your credit cards. Make sure the one you keep is accepted widely, and use it wisely and sparingly.

Simple Budgets

If you have a complicated method of trying to keep track of how much you spent where, look for an easier budgeting arrangement. Here are a few budget types that are easy to work with:

The envelope system, the most complete method, is taught by an agency in my community that provides money management counseling service. It is especially good for persons who have difficulty tracking where their money has gone.

The system has three parts: a checking account, a savings account, and envelopes for cash payments. The checking account is used for fixed monthly expenses: rent, utilities, debt payments, and monthly contributions to your church and to charities such as the United Way. The savings account is for periodic bills (quarterly, semi-annual, or annual) and for emergency expenses. Include here also Christmas and other gift-giving, home maintenance and car repairs, vacations, and back-to-school expenses. Lastly, use separate envelopes for each of the categories that requires ready cash—food, gasoline, entertainment, allowances, personal and household cleaning products (bar and laundry soaps, toothpaste), and miscellaneous needs (stationery supplies).

The advantage of this plan is that it enables you to see in detail where your discretionary funds are being spent. People generally decrease their spending on the envelope items thirty percent by using this system, the agency says, freeing up money for their savings account where it can ease and de-stress their budget.

• *The direct deposit method* is the one my family uses. It is similar to the above except that we deposit all of our income into two accounts: a joint checking account, which we use for monthly and cash operating expenses, and a savings account for periodic bills, travel money, emergency needs, and to accumulate savings for investment purposes.

This method leaves us short of operating cash, but we like that because it discourages us from overspending. For operating cash, we overwrite the checks at our local grocery store and supplement that with small checks that come in from my writing business and a few dividends we receive from investment funds. Those of you who like this option could use automatic teller machines as your supplement. If you do, make certain you record your withdrawals.

• *The check + cash plan.* An accountant friend of ours deposits into a checking account sufficient funds to cover all fixed expenses, maintaining a sizeable balance to cover the periodic bills. He takes the rest in cash to use for the family's discretionary spending—groceries, clothes, gas for the car, et cetera.

Whichever method you use, remain flexible. A budget is just a guide. Make yours a servant, not a straitjacket. If an unforeseen opportunity comes along that justifies breaking your guidelines, go for it. One of our daughters had an opportunity to study at a summer music school during her high school years. The cost was beyond our budget, but we extended ourselves a bit. She went, and it changed her career goal and the course of her college studies.

Lean on the Lord's Providence

Finally, and of greatest import, depend on God to lead you financially on your path through life. Regardless of how well we insure our assets, regardless of how hard we try to maintain adequate emergency savings and invest for future needs, life holds no guarantees. The unexpected can wipe out the best-laid plans.

God alone is our best security. God knows what is best for us and our families. He knows what will make us happy. God also has promised to take care of us: "Do not worry about your life, what you will eat or what you will drink, or about your body, what you will wear . . . your heavenly Father knows that you need all these things. But strive first for the kingdom of God and his righteousness, and all these things will be given to you as well" (Matthew 6:25, 32-33).

God's recipe for economic and spiritual satisfaction is simple: "Do not store up for yourselves treasures on earth, where moth and rust consume and where thieves break in and steal; but store up for yourselves treasures in heaven, where neither moth nor rust consumes and where thieves do not break in and steal. For where your treasure is, there your heart will be also" (Matthew 6:19-21).

The happiest people I saw on my trip to Mexico were not the wealthy merchants and government officials in Mexico City. The happiest people were the peasants in the small villages whose means were poor by the standards of the developed world, but who had all they needed to live a full, rewarding life—enough food, a roof over their heads, a church on the hilltop as the focus of their spiritual lives, music in their hearts and homes (they all seemed to own audiotapes), a rich community life, families and friends to share life's joys and sorrows, and many festivals by which to celebrate life. Missionaries from my community found the same joyful way of life in Paraguay.

Like these happy Mexican and Paraguayan villagers, be content with what you have and celebrate *your* life.

21

Live Life to the Fullest!

"The strength and the happiness of a man [or woman] consists in finding out the way in which God is going, and going in that way too."
——Henry Ward Beecher

I've thrown a lot of challenges at you in this book. I have encouraged you to realize the most from your life and to make each moment count. I have urged you to make God a daily partner in your life. I have suggested a number of ways to control your time so that it doesn't control you. And I have advised you to build and maintain positive whole health habits and attitudes.

Family is uppermost in the lives of almost all women. I hope I have shown you how to make your time with your family valuable and rewarding—not just by spending it meaningfully, but also by minimizing or condensing the rest of your at-home workload. Finally, since money makes the world turn, I have advocated a financially controlled and restrained lifestyle as another vitally important way to de-stress your life and enjoy it more.

Many of the suggestions and ideas in this book may sound attractive to you, but it is one thing to wish for them and quite another to act on your desires and put them in place. Action means change. It takes courage to risk change. It takes time—time to plan, to prioritize, and to implement new behaviors. And it takes patience—the ultimate in patience—to establish new patterns that will do a better job for you.

Don't lose heart. Keep trying. The new patterns will gradually come.

Here are some tips to assist you on your journey:

1. *Be serious about your goals.* Do you *really* want a more relaxed, yet full and rich work, family, and personal life? If you do, then be willing to work on it.

2. *Take one step at a time.* Don't try to implement all the ideas that look workable to you at one time. Try the most compelling one first. Once you feel comfortable there, look for your next most desired change and work on that, and so forth. Mountains are climbed one step at a time.

3. *View yourself as successful.* Researchers have found that imagining what could happen to you actually fires the nervous system the same way as doing it would. When a golfer tells himself *not* to hit a ball into the water, his mind pictures the ball going into the water. Consequently it is more likely to happen.

Avoid negative imaging. Focus on what you *want* to occur. Your chance for success is much greater.

4. *Do it YOUR way.* Other people can throw all kinds of challenges in your lap, but only you know how to make things work for you. You may have even better techniques and ideas than those presented here. Dig with your own shovel. You'll be more successful, and you may find buried treasure.

5. *Learn from your mistakes.* Whenever we try something new, we are bound to make mistakes. Disappointment follows. But failure is merely a step up toward getting where we want to go. Thomas Edison was mocked for unsuccessfully trying twelve hundred materials for the filament of his great dream—the incandescent light bulb. "You have failed twelve hundred times," someone told him. "I have discovered twelve hundred materials that don't work," he replied.

6. *Persevere.* Where would society be today if Edison had

stopped trying? People who persist have a habit of making their goals and dreams come true. You can, too.

Habits and attitudes are hard to change, but what have you to lose except a bunch of old habits that are not very comfortable or satisfying at times? What have you to gain? A lightened, more relaxed, more enjoyable life.

Living light and easy does not mean that we bypass the pain and vexation of human existence. Unfortunately, we can't avoid it, and we can't walk around it. What we can do is to walk through it serenely, come what may, by surrendering our total lives and destiny into the hands of God.

When we walk a life surrendered to God, the roughest roads do not undo us. God's road is paved with unconditional love and undergirded by unfailing support. It is a road with a constant view of the horizon, one with a brighter hereafter. On that road, everything that happens has a purpose, and all things work one way or another for our benefit. So, on the spiritual front also, how can we lose?

This level of spiritual maturity does not come easily. It takes time and tremendous courage to decide to surrender our all to God. When we do, God does not disappoint us.

That is the way to live life to the fullest. "Take delight in the LORD, and he will give you the desires of your heart" (Psalm 37:4).

In Closing . . .

I hope you have found some ideas in this book worth pursuing. I hope I have given you sufficient reason and the motivation to attempt them. And I hope, in so doing, you will find that they lighten and enrich your life.

Most of all, my friend, I hope that you have seen throughout this book how living your life with God at the helm will assure you the greatest and most certain peace of mind and heart.

To that end, God bless.